PUPPET SCRIPTS BY THE SITUATION

Margaret Cheasebro

Broadm
Nashville

D1367931

To
Wally, my husband,
whose patient understanding of my need to write
helped make this book possible
Philip, my son,
who has added a whole new dimension
of love and inspiration to my life

© Copyright 1989 • Broadman Press
All rights reserved
4275-27

ISBN: 0-8054-7527-3
Dewey Decimal Classification: 791.5
Subject Heading: PUPPETS AND PUPPET PLAYS
Library of Congress Catalog Card Number: 88-7537

Printed in the United States of America

Library of Congress Cataloging-in-Publication Data

Cheasebro, Margaret, 1945-
  Puppet scripts by the situation.

  1. Puppets and puppet-plays in Christian
education.   I. Title.
BV1535.9.P8C53   1989   246'.7   88-7537
ISBN 0-8054-7527-3 (pbk.)

6554

Contents

1
Your Best Friend Stops Liking You

Scripture: Ephesians 4:32
Props: Gift (It can be an imaginary one.)
Performance Time: 8 minutes
Characters: Jill, Monica, Mrs. Turnbull, Rachel, Monica's mother

(*On the playground.*)
(*Jill and Monica enter center stage.*)
Jill: Let's play jump rope, Monica.
Monica: OK. I'll get Rachel to help you turn the rope while I jump.
Jill: But you jumped first last time. It's my turn now.
Monica: All right, Crabby, you jump first.
Jill: I'm not crabby.
Monica (*calls out*): Rachel, want to play jump rope?
Rachel (*appears stage left*): Sure.
Monica: Here, you help Jill turn the rope.
Jill: But you said I could jump first.
Monica: Oh, all right. Help me turn, Rachel.
Rachel: OK.
(*Rachel stands left, Monica stands right. They pretend to turn an invisible rope as Jill jumps in the middle. After only three jumps, Jill misses.*)
Monica: You goofed, Jill. Now it's my turn.
Jill: But I only jumped three times.
Monica: You'll get another turn. Here, take my end.

Jill (*grumpily*): OK. (*She takes Monica's place. Monica jumps and jumps.*)

Jill: Aren't you ever going to stop and give Rachel a turn?

Monica: As soon as I miss.

Jill: At this rate, that could take forever.

Rachel: I don't mind. It's kind of fun turning the rope.

Jill: Well, I mind. If Monica doesn't give you a turn, I'll never get one.

Monica: Quit arguing and watch me. Don't you think I'm a great jumper?

Jill: I can't believe how conceited you are!

Monica: Bug off, Jill. You'll get another turn. I won't let you down. After all, I'm your friend, aren't I?

Jill: I suppose so.

(*Bell rings.*)

Rachel: Oops! There's the bell. Recess is over. (*She drops the rope and exits left. Monica has stopped jumping, and Jill is holding the other end of the rope.*).

Jill: See what you've done, you hog? You took up the whole recess with your jumping. I'm not going to turn the jump rope for you again.

Monica: See if I care, Miss Always-Wants-Her-Own-Way. Since you're being so nasty, I'm not going to invite you to my birthday party on Saturday.

Jill: So what? Who wants to go to your party, anyway? You'll probably hog all the refreshments and win all the games just to make yourself feel great.

Monica: I never heard such stupid talk before. Some best friend you turned out to be. (*Monica exits right.*)

Jill: Who cares about her party? I don't care if I never see her again. (*Exits left.*)

(*Walking to school two days later.*)

(*Rachel and Jill enter together at stage left.*)

Rachel: Isn't it exciting about Monica's birthday party? What present will you get her?

Jill: None! I haven't been invited.

Rachel: You're kidding! You're her best friend. Maybe she thought you knew you were automatically invited.

Jill: No. Monica doesn't like me anymore.

Rachel: Why? You've been best friends since kindergarten.

Jill: Not anymore. She hasn't spoken to me since that day when we played jump rope at recess.

Rachel: I remember. You got mad at her for jumping too long.

Jill: And for telling us how great she was and that I'd get another turn, which was a lie. You didn't even get to jump at all.

Rachel: I didn't mind. I think it's more fun to turn the rope. Besides, I'm kind of a lousy jumper.

Jill· I like to jump.

Rachel: It's sad you two are mad at each other over a little thing like that.

Jill: Do you call telling the world how great you are, lying, and hogging the jump rope a little thing? And something else: She told a bunch of kids not to play with me anymore because I'm mean.

Rachel: Compared to a lot of things, those are little.

Jill: Compared to what?

Rachel: Things like stealing everything from your desk, running into you with a bicycle, or tearing up your homework so you'll get an *F.*

Jill: I suppose. But it's still a big deal to me. If Monica's not going to invite me to her party and doesn't want me for a friend anymore, fine. I'll just find another best friend.

Rachel: Good luck. Best friends are hard to find. See you at recess. (*Exits right.*)

Jill: Yeah, see you at recess. I might as well not even go out for recess. No one will play with me. (*Exits right.*)

(*On the playground.*)
(*Jill enters center. Stands around doing nothing. Mrs. Turnbull enters at right.*)

Mrs. Turnbull: Hi, Jill. Why aren't you playing with your friends?

Jill: They won't let me.

Mrs. Turnbull: Why?

Jill: Monica told them not to play with me because I'm mean.

Mrs. Turnbull: But Monica is your best friend. Why would she say something like that?

Jill: We got mad at each other a couple of days ago. She doesn't like me anymore.

Mrs. Turnbull: I'm so sorry, Jill. That must hurt you very much.

Jill: I don't care! I'll just find another best friend.

Mrs. Turnbull: Don't give up on Monica. She probably feels bad about this too.

Jill: She doesn't care. She didn't even invite me to her birthday party.

Mrs. Turnbull: Oops! I've got to go. Someone's calling for help. (*Exits right.*)

Jill (*sniffles*): I miss Monica even if she does think she's so great.

Rachel (*enters right*): Quick, Jill! There's been an accident. Run to the principal's office and tell Mr. Oglethorpe to call for an ambulance.

Jill: What happened?

Rachel: Monica fell off the monkey bars. Her right arm is bent real funny. Mrs. Turnbull thinks it's broken.

Jill: Oh, no! I'll run as fast as I can. (*Both exit left.*)

(*Next day on the playground.*)

(*Jill and Rachel enter together from right.*)

Jill: How's Monica?

Rachel: Not too good. It was a bad break. She's got a big cast on her arm. She can't write or do anything with her right hand.

Jill: Then I guess she'll be out of school for a while, especially since she's right-handed.

Rachel: Yeah. Her parents called off her big birthday party. They're just going to have a family get-together at home since Monica doesn't feel well.

Jill: That's too bad.

Rachel: You know what I think is really too bad?

Jill: What?

Rachel: That you and Monica still aren't speaking. I know you like her.

Jill: I'd speak to her, but she told me she didn't want to be my friend anymore.

Rachel: I don't think she really meant it.

Jill: I do.

Rachel: Well, even if she did, you could tell her how sorry you are about her arm.

Jill: I really am sorry she broke her arm, but she probably wouldn't speak to me.

Rachel: I'll bet she would.

Jill: I'll think about it.

(Bell rings.)

Rachel: There's the end of recess bell. See you later. *(Both exit left.)*

(The next day after school.)

Jill *(enters right)*: Hey, Rachel, come here.

Rachel *(enters left)*: Hi, Jill.

Jill: See this? *(Holds up a present.)*

Rachel: What is it?

Jill: A present.

Rachel: Who's it for? Me?

Jill: No, Silly. Guess again.

Rachel: For your boyfriend.

Jill: No, Goofy. I don't have a boyfriend.

Rachel: For the teacher, to butter her up.

Jill: No! Mrs. Turnbull is so nice I don't need to butter her up.

Rachel: I give up. Who's it for?

Jill: It's for Monica.

Rachel: Are you two friends again?

Jill: No, but I decided if she's going to miss having her big birthday party, she's probably sad. Even though she doesn't want to be my friend anymore, I still want to be her friend. So after school today, I'm going to take the present to her house.

Rachel: That's a great idea. I'm glad you're going to try to be friends again with Monica.

Jill: I've got to get over to Monica's house. See you later. (*Both exit center.*)

(*At Monica's house later that day.*)

Jill (*enters right*): Knock, knock.

Monica's mother (*enters left*): Hello, Jill. How nice to see you. Come in.

Jill: I came to see Monica.

Monica's mother: She'll be glad. You're the only friend who's visited her since the accident.

Jill: I am?

Monica's mother: That's right. Wait here, and I'll get Monica. (*Exits left.*)

Jill: I can hardly believe I'm the only one who's visited Monica. I thought everyone but me would have been here.

Monica (*enters slowly from left*): Hi, Jill.

Jill: Hi, Monica. I'm sorry about your accident.

Monica: Me too. But I'm getting better.

Jill: I brought you a birthday present.

Monica: You did?

Jill: Here it is. (*Hands her the present.*)

Monica: Thanks. That was nice of you.

Jill: I wanted you to have a little fun on your birthday since you can't have your party.

Monica: I'm sorry I didn't invite you to my party. I was acting like a real klunkhead. You're my best friend. My party wouldn't have been the same without you.

Jill: Am I still your best friend?

Monica: Of course, Silly. I hope I'm still your best friend too.

Jill: You are.

Monica: I'm glad. I really missed having you to play with.

Jill: But you told everyone not to play with me.

Monica: I know. It was stupid. Will you forgive me?

Jill: I already have.

Monica: Thanks. Let's go show Mom what you gave me.

Jill: All right.

Monica: And maybe on my birthday tomorrow, Mom and Dad will let you come over to have ice cream and cake with us.

(*Both exit left.*)

2
You Think Nobody Loves You

Scripture: 1 Samuel 16:7
Props: None
Performance Time: 15 minutes
Characters: Jason, Kenneth, Peter, Howard, Mr. Willowby

(*On the playground.*)
(*Jason and Kenneth enter center stage.*)
Jason: Fe, fi, fo, fum, Peter McAdams is stupid and dumb.
Kenneth: Hey, that rhymes.
Jason: Thanks. It sounds so good I'll say it again. Fe, fi (*Kenneth joins in*), fo, fum, Peter McAdams is stupid and dumb. Fe, fi (*Kenneth suddenly stops, while Jason continues with a couple more words of the rhyme.*)
Kenneth: Wait a minute. Why are we saying Peter McAdams is stupid and dumb?
Jason: Because he is. You know Peter. He's always stumbling over his own shoes, and he can't read very well. Listening to him in class is so funny. I almost die laughing at the way he mixes up words.
Kenneth: He tries, though. The teacher says he's pretty smart. He just has trouble with reading and with falling over his own two feet.
Jason: I call that stupid and dumb. Fe, fi, fo, fum, Peter McAdams . . .(*Peter enters stage left.*)
Kenneth: Sh-h-h-h! Here comes Peter.
Jason: Oops!

Kenneth: Hi, Peter.

Peter (*sadly*): Hi. (*Trips as he walks toward them.*)

Kenneth: What's wrong?

Peter: I heard you two singing about how stupid and dumb I am.

Jason: You know me, Peter. I just like to make up funny rhymes.

Peter: That one wasn't funny. Why do you guys always pick on me?

Kenneth: We don't.

Peter: Jason does. He hates me, don't you, Jason?

Jason: No, I don't. I just think you're a real pain sometimes. (*Laughs.*)

Kenneth: Jason! That's no way to talk.

Jason: It's true. Fe, fi, fo, fum, Peter McAdams is a pain and a bum.

Kenneth: You're the pain, Jason. I don't think you're so bad, Peter. In fact, I think you're OK.

Peter: You're just saying that to make me feel better.

Kenneth: No, honest. I mean it!

Jason (*laughs*): You're a real card, Kenneth. If you really think Peter is OK, then choose him to be on your team the next time we play volleyball.

Kenneth: Well, uh, sure. OK. I will.

Peter: You don't have to. I know whoever has me on their team always loses.

Kenneth: That's silly, and to prove it I will definitely make sure you get on my team the next game we play.

Peter: You mean it?

Kenneth: Sure.

Jason: I like to win, so I'll be sure to be on the other team.

Kenneth: You do that. We don't need a big mouth like you.

Jason: Watch what you say, Kenneth Nelson, or I'll start making up rhymes about you.

Kenneth: Sticks and stones may break my bones, but your rhymes will never hurt me.

Jason: You're going to lose, Kenneth. Why don't you pick better friends than Peter the Klutz?

Kenneth: Get out of here!

Jason: My pleasure. (*He exits center.*)

Peter: Wow, Kenneth, nobody ever stood up for me like that before.

Kenneth: Jason's a real bully. I couldn't stand to let him call you names.

Peter: It's OK. I'm used to it. Most people don't like me.

Kenneth: I think you're fine.

Peter: Thanks. You're the only friend I've got.

(*Howard enters left.*)

Howard: Hi, Kenneth. Hi, Peter.

Kenneth and Peter: Hi.

Howard: Have you heard about the volleyball tournament?

Kenneth: No.

Peter: Me neither.

Howard: It's the principal's idea. He was given some special tickets to see the Olympic volleyball team play next week.

Kenneth: Wow! Volleyball is my favorite sport.

Peter: Neat! I can't play very well, but I like to try.

Howard: Mr. Willowby has only eight tickets. So he wants all of us who want to go to divide up into teams of eight players. Then we'll have a tournament tomorrow. The winning team gets to see the Olympic team play.

Kenneth: I sure would like to watch them play.

Peter: Me too.

Howard: Then you'd better get to the principal's office quick and sign up.

Kenneth: Let's go, Peter. (*All three exit left.*)

(*On the playground later that day.*)

(*Kenneth and Jason enter together on left.*)

Jason: Did you sign up for the volleyball tournament?

Kenneth: I sure did.

Jason: Me too. I'd give up making rhymes for a whole year if I could see the Olympic team play.

(*Howard enters right.*)

Howard: Hey, Kenneth, guess what?

Kenneth: What?

Howard: You've been chosen as captain of one of the three tournament teams.

Kenneth: I have?

Howard: Yes. The principal chose one captain for each team. That means you and the other captains get to choose who's going to be on your team.

Kenneth: Who do we choose from?

Howard: From the people who signed up to play.

Jason: Did Peter sign up?

Howard: He sure did.

Jason: That's a scream, Kenneth. It's so funny. (*Laughs.*)

Kenneth: I don't see anything funny about Peter signing up.

Jason: Well, I do. Remember what you told Peter you'd do?

Kenneth: What?

Jason: You told him you'd choose him to be on your team the next volleyball game you played just to show him the team he's on doesn't always lose.

Kenneth: Ulp. That's right, I did.

Howard: That was a dumb thing to say. You know what a klutz Peter is. He fouls up everything.

Kenneth: I know. But I already promised I'd choose him. On the other hand, I didn't know about the tournament when I said that. But if I don't choose him, he'll be even more sure everybody hates him. What am I going to do?

Jason: Listen to my rhymes more carefully next time. I warned you. Remember? Fe, fi, fo, fum, Peter McAdams is stupid and dumb.

Kenneth: Oh, shut up!

Jason: Fibbledy, fobbledy, fubbledy, fuse, Kenneth Nelson is going to lose.

Kenneth: You're a real pain, Jason. Go pedal your rhymes somewhere else.

Howard: Got to go, guys. I have to tell everyone else about the captains. You two quit arguing, OK? (*He exits right.*)

Jason: I can hardly wait to see how badly Peter fouls up your team.

Kenneth: Get lost!

Jason: Don't pick me for your team. If you do, I'll refuse to be on it. I'm not going to play with that klutz Peter. (*Jason and Kenneth exit center.*)

(*Peter enters left.*)

Peter: I heard them talking about me. Everyone hates me. I knew it all along. Even Kenneth. I want to see the Olympic team play so badly. But if I play in the tournament, I'll ruin Kenneth's chance of going. What am I going to do? (*He thinks a moment.*) I know. I'll ask the principal to take my name off the list. Then Kenneth won't have to choose me. (*He runs to stage right.*) Knock, knock. Mr. Willowby, are you in your office?

Mr. Willowby (*from off stage right*): Who is it?

Peter: Peter McAdams.

Mr. Willowby (*enters stage right*): Hi, Peter. How are you?

Peter: Fine. I came to ask if I can take my name off the list of players.

Mr. Willowby: It's too late. The list has already been typed up and is circulating among the three captains. In fact, they're choosing their teams right now.

Peter: But I've got to get my name off that list.

Mr. Willowby: Why?

Peter: Because.

Mr. Willowby: Because why?

Peter: Just because.

Mr. Willowby: I know desperation when I see it. Tell me what the problem is.

Peter: Well, see, I'm, well, you know, Sir, I'm a . . . klutz.

Mr. Willowby: You're not the only one who isn't a super athlete. But that's no reason to take your name off the list.

Peter: You don't understand. Kenneth promised he'd choose me to play on his team next time there was a volleyball game so he could convince me the team I'm on doesn't always lose.

But he didn't know about the tournament when he made that promise.

Mr. Willowby: And now he thinks he has to choose you.

Peter: Yes, and if he does, his team will lose, and he won't get to see the Olympic team play.

Mr. Willowby: Peter, there are three teams competing against each other. Kenneth might not win even if you aren't on his team.

Peter: But he'd have a better chance if I didn't play.

Mr. Willowby: Don't be too sure about that. I think you may be selling yourself short.

Peter: Please, Mr. Willowby, I have to get my name off that list.

Mr. Willowby: No, Peter. I'm not going to let you take it off the list. I think you may learn something special about yourself by playing in the tournament.

Peter (*discouraged*): Yes, Sir.

(*Mr. Willowby exits right.*)

Peter: Now Kenneth will hate me even more. What am I going to do? I wish I were dead. (*He walks disheartenedly back and forth across the stage, tripping over his own feet once or twice.*) Maybe if I hid somewhere, no one could find me. Then I couldn't play in the tournament. That's it! I'll gather a supply of food and water and go hide until the tournament is over. (*He runs toward stage left.*)

(*Kenneth enters stage right.*)

Kenneth: Wait, Peter.

Peter: Peter's not here. (*Trips and falls.*) Oops! What a lousy time to trip.

Kenneth (*approaches Peter and helps him up*): You goofy guy. What do you mean Peter's not here? You're Peter, and you're here.

Peter: Yeah, well, I guess I am.

Kenneth: Guess what?

Peter: You picked me for your team, and now you're going to lose the tournament.

Kenneth: You're half right. I picked you for my team, but we're not going to lose.

Peter: You don't know that.

Kenneth: I have a plan that I think might work.

Peter: You're dreaming.

Kenneth: Do you want to see the Olympic team play or not?

Peter: Sure I do.

Kenneth: Then listen to my plan.

Peter: OK. I'm listening.

Kenneth: First, I want you to know something you don't understand about yourself.

Peter: You mean there's something I don't understand about myself?

Kenneth: That's right. You think you're a klutz and stupid and dumb. But what you really are is funny.

Peter: Funny?

Kenneth: Yeah. You make people laugh.

Peter: I do?

Kenneth: Yes. You look real funny when you stumble and trip.

Peter: I know. People are always laughing at me.

Kenneth: That's because you know how to make them laugh. You're a born clown and don't even know it.

Peter: I am?

Kenneth: Yes. And that's what you're going to be on our team.

Peter: A clown?

Kenneth: A clown.

Peter: I've never seen a clown on a volleyball team before.

Kenneth: Then you're going to make history.

Peter: I guess I could give it a try.

Kenneth: Good boy! I want you to fall over your feet as you pretend to try and reach the ball.

Peter: That won't be hard.

Kenneth: The idea is to make the other teams laugh so hard they won't be able to concentrate on the game.

Peter: You really think I can make them laugh that hard?

Kenneth: Yes, and the audience will think you're so funny they'll

want our team to win. They'll cheer for us, and that will help
us try harder. It's easier to play well when people are cheering
for you.

Peter: That's a really strange plan. But if it will give you a chance
to win, I'll do it.

Kenneth: Great! Come on, let's practice, so you can get good at
clowning around without getting in the way of people trying
to hit the ball. We can't tell anyone about our plan, OK? It's
got to be a secret, or it won't work. (*Both exit right.*)

(*On the playground the next day.*)
(*Mr. Willowby enters left and watches as Peter, on stage right,
practices tripping over his own two feet.*)

Mr. Willowby: Peter, are you all right?

Peter: Oh, hi, Mr. Willowby. Yeah, I'm fine.

Mr. Willowby: I never saw you trip quite so much.

Peter: Oh, uh, I guess I'm a little extra klutzy today.

Mr. Willowby: Well, be careful. I wouldn't want you to hurt
yourself before the tournament today.

Peter: Thanks. I'll try to be more careful.

(*Mr. Willowby exits left.*)

Peter: Whew, that was close. (*He looks around.*) No one else is in
sight. I think I can practice my clown act safely now. (*He
trips some more.*)

(*Jason enters left.*)

Jason: Well, if it isn't Peter McAdams stumbling over his own
feet again. Are you practicing to help your team lose today?

Peter: I'm practicing, all right.

Jason: If you ever learn how to walk straight, let me know, and
I'll enter you in a circus—as a clown. (*Laughs.*)

Peter: Clowns aren't so bad. Have a nice day, Jason.

Jason: I will because my team is going to win. (*He exits left.*)

Peter: I'll show him! He's not going to win if I can help it.

(*Howard enters left.*)

Howard: Peter, Mr. Willowby told me to round up all the players.
The tournament is about to begin.

Peter: I'm ready.

Howard: You sound excited.

Peter: I am.

Howard: That's funny. Kenneth was excited too when I saw him earlier today. You guys don't have something up your sleeve, do you?

Peter: You know me. I couldn't keep something up my sleeve if I tried. I'm too much of a klutz.

Howard: Ha, ha, that's a good one. Come on, we'll meet back here after the tournament, and Mr. Willowby will give the tickets to the winners. (*Both exit right.*)

(*On the playground after the tournament.*)

(*Howard, Jason, Kenneth, and Mr. Willowby enter stage right.*)

Mr. Willowby (*laughing*): I've never seen anything so funny in all my life.

Kenneth: I laughed so hard I could hardly hit the ball.

Jason: Maybe that's why your team lost and mine won.

Kenneth: Maybe. But we had lots of fun.

Howard: Who would have thought that Peter the Klutz could become Peter the Clown?

Jason: It's revolting! Now I'm going to have to change all my rhymes.

Mr. Willowby: By the way, where is Peter?

Kenneth: I don't know. He looked real discouraged when we lost the tournament. He walked off by himself.

Mr. Willowby: Go find him. I've got good news for him and for everyone else too.

Howard: You do? Tell us what it is.

Mr. Willowby: Not till Peter gets here. He's largely responsible for my very good news.

Kenneth: I'll look for him. (*All exit right.*)

(*Elsewhere on the playground.*)

(*Kenneth enters right.*)

Kenneth: Peter, where are you? I've got good news for you. Please, Peter, if you're hiding, come out. (*He walks across stage as he calls to Peter.*) I hear something like a rustling sound. Is that you, Peter? (*He goes to left edge of stage, pulls Peter from behind curtain.*) Peter, what were you doing behind that bush?

Peter: I was hiding.

Kenneth: Why?

Peter: So no one would find me.

Kenneth: But we're all looking for you.

Peter: I made such a fool of myself on the volleyball court, and I got in everybody's way. I think I made everyone on my team miss the ball.

Kenneth: I think so too, but it was so funny. Everyone laughed and laughed.

Peter: I know. They were all laughing at me.

Kenneth: That's just it, Peter. You made them laugh. They thought you were funny.

Peter: But I wanted you to win.

Kenneth: That doesn't matter now. I knew you were a born clown, and you proved it today.

Peter: If you say so.

Kenneth: I know you don't believe me, but it's true. Come on. Mr. Willowby sent me to get you. He says he has good news for everyone.

Peter: He does?

Kenneth: Yes. Now, are you coming?

Peter: OK. But can I walk behind you? I don't want anyone to see me.

Kenneth: Don't be silly. Everyone wants to see you. You're a hero.

Peter: I am not. Quit trying to cheer me up.

Kenneth: It's true. Your problem is you don't know what a neat person you really are. Now, come.

Peter: OK. (*Both exit left.*)

(*On the playground immediately afterwards.*)
(*Howard, Jason, and Mr. Willowby enter stage right.*)
Mr. Willowby: Where could Peter and Kenneth be?

Howard: Want me to look for them?

Mr. Willowby: No, let's give them a few more minutes.

Jason: Peter probably tripped over his own two feet and knocked himself out.

Mr. Willowby (*worriedly*): I hope not.

Jason: Just kidding.

(*Kenneth and Peter enter stage right.*)

Kenneth: Hey, everyone, I found Peter.

Mr. Willowby: Wonderful!

Howard: Hi, Peter.

Jason (*mumbling*): Yeah, hi, Peter.

Peter (*walks behind Kenneth*): Hi.

Mr. Willowby: All of you, gather round. I have wonderful news.

Kenneth: What is it?

Mr. Willowby: Before I tell you, I want Peter to come stand beside me.

(*Peter crouches behind Kenneth.*)

Kenneth (*turns to Peter*): Go on, Peter.

(*Peter nervously walks toward Mr. Willowby, who stands near stage left.*)

Mr. Willowby: Come, Son, stand right here. I'm proud of you. (*Peter stands beside Mr. Willowby, and they both face the other three students.*) Do you know why I'm proud of you?

Peter: No, Sir.

Mr. Willowby: Because you did your very best on the volleyball court today.

Peter: I was a klutz. I made my team lose.

Jason: You sure did. Just like I said you would.

Mr. Willowby: Quiet, Jason. I'll deal with you later.

Jason: Yes, Sir.

Mr. Willowby: You were a clown, Peter. You made everyone laugh. I even laughed so hard I almost fell off my chair.

Peter: You did?

Mr. Willowby: Yes. Everyone thought you were so funny that someone told the Olympic team about our tournament and your performance.

Peter: They did?

Mr. Willowby: Yes.

Howard: Wow!

Kenneth: Neat!

Jason: Now I've heard everything.

Mr. Willowby: They were so impressed that they're going to come to our school.

Peter, Howard, Kenneth, and Jason: Our school?

Mr. Willowby: And play a game for everyone in the school to see.

Peter, Howard, Kenneth, and Jason: Yay, hooray, whoopee!

Mr. Willowby: And they especially want to meet you, Peter.

Peter: They do?

Mr. Willowby: Yes. They said they might even be able to learn a thing or two from you.

Howard: You're a hero, Peter.

Kenneth: I knew you were a born clown.

Mr. Willowby: I had a feeling you'd discover something special about yourself if you played in the tournament. I just didn't know how special that something was going to be.

Peter: I don't know what to say.

Mr. Willowby: Tell us what you discovered about yourself.

Peter: Well, uh, I discovered that being a klutz isn't so bad after all.

Mr. Willowby: And I think you've taught us that we can turn our worst traits into something good if we do our best.

Jason: For you, Peter, I've created a new rhyme.

Kenneth: Bug off, Jason. We're sick of your rhymes.

Howard: Yeah, just keep your mouth shut.

Jason: Wait, this is a good one.

Kenneth: OK, but if it isn't, we'll lock you in your room when the Olympic team comes.

Jason: Here it is. Fiddle, faddle, fuddle, flown, Peter McAdams is a first-rate clown.

Howard: All right!

Kenneth: Yay, Peter!

Mr. Willowby: Everyone loves Peter.

(*All exit left.*)

3
You Get a Failing Grade

Scripture: Proverbs 4:13

Props: None. Paper exchanges hands between teacher and students, but it can be imaginary.

Performance Time: 10 minutes

Characters: David, Frank, Mrs. Allen, Emily, Mary

(*On school playground.*)

(*David and Frank enter, center stage.*)

David: Want to shoot baskets after school, Frank?

Frank: I'd like to, but I have to go home and study for our social studies test tomorrow.

David: The test is a piece of cake. Stay and play basketball.

Frank: Sorry. I really have to study.

David: What a party pooper you are. Can't you ever stop studying and have a little fun?

Frank: Hey, klunkhead, let's review a little history. Who went to the movies with you last Saturday?

David: You, but . . .

Frank: And who went bicycling with you after school yesterday?

David: You. But that's . . .

Frank: And who invited you over to spend the night two weekends ago and stayed up till midnight playing Sorry, Dominoes, and Crazy Eights with you?

David: You, but that's different.

Frank: No, it isn't. You're a great friend, David, and I like to do things with you. But I've really got to study for this test.

David: Why? You always get *A*s.

Frank: No, I don't. I got a *C* on my social studies written report.

David: The one on Belgium?

Frank: Yeah. And you know why?

David: Why?

Frank: Because I let you talk me into playing computer games at your house after school two days in a row when I should have been doing my report.

David: So now you're blaming me.

Frank: No, I'm blaming myself. I have to make an *A* on that test tomorrow to bring up the *C* I got on that report.

David: *C* sounds pretty good to me. I got an *F*.

Frank: I know. You reported on Germany, and your entire report was one page of messy handwriting.

David: Well, I learned something from it.

Frank: No kidding.

David: Really, I learned how to say some German words from World War II.

Frank: What words?

David: Hiyo, Silver.

Frank: What?

David: Uh, I mean, *Heil* Hitler.

Frank: You're crazy.

David: Well, they sound about the same to me.

Frank: You're a goon if I ever saw one.

David: So stay and play basketball with a goon.

Frank: Sorry. You'd better study for that test too, or you'll get an *F* on it just like you did on your report.

(*Frank exits center.*)

David: What does he know? If he won't play with me, I'll shoot baskets by myself. (*David exits center.*)

(*In the classroom.*)

(*Mrs. Allen enters stage left. David, Frank, Mary, and Emily enter on right. Mrs. Allen stands facing the four students.*)

Mrs. Allen: All right, students, time is up. I will come and collect your papers now. (*She moves to Emily.*) I see you have all the blank spaces filled in, Emily. I hope they're filled in with the right answers.

Emily: Me too. I studied real hard.

Mrs. Allen: Good for you. (*She moves to Frank.*) What a neat looking paper, Frank. I'm looking for an excellent grade from you.

Frank: Thank you, Mrs. Allen. I tried my best.

Mrs. Allen: That's all I can ask for. (*She moves to Mary.*) I see a few blanks on your page, Mary.

Mary: Yes, Ma'am. I didn't know the answers to some of the questions.

Mrs. Allen: Did you study?

Mary: Yes, but I guess I could have done better.

Mrs. Allen: You need a good grade on this test to bring up your average.

Mary: I know.

Mrs. Allen: We'll hope for the best. I'm going to grade these right away. (*She moves to David.*) David, why is your paper blank?

David: Because I didn't know any of the answers.

Mrs. Allen: Why didn't you know any of the answers, David?

David: I guess because I didn't study hard enough.

Mrs. Allen: I think it's because you didn't study at all.

David: But I did!

Mrs. Allen: I saw you playing basketball after school yesterday. If you'd used that time to study, you might have known some of the answers.

David: But, Mrs. Allen, I did study. Honest!

Mrs. Allen: If you really studied, you'll know the answer to this easy question. And if you can answer it, I'll give you a chance to take the test over. Maybe you just had a bad morning.

David: OK!

Mrs. Allen: What was the name of President George Washington's wife?

David: That's easy. Uh, it was, wait, I know. Sure! It was Mrs. First Lady Washington.

(*Other three children snicker.*)

Mrs. Allen: Quiet. You'll have to do better than that, David. Tell me her first name.

David: Uh, well, I, that is, I guess I don't know.

Mrs. Allen: That's what I thought. You didn't study at all, did you?

David (*subdued*): No, Ma'am.

Mrs. Allen: Class, tell David the name of George Washington's wife.

Frank, Mary, and Emily: Martha.

Mrs. Allen: That's right. Now, all of you, go out to recess while I grade your tests. When you come back in, I'll tell you whether you've passed social studies for the year.

(*Frank, David, Mary, and Emily exit right. Mrs. Allen grades imaginary papers. She smiles at some papers, shakes her head in discouragement at others, and makes flourishing marks on each paper as though marking an answer. The bell rings. All four children return and take their places.*)

Mrs. Allen: I have the test results and your final grades. I want each of you to come here when I call your name, and I'll tell you what you got so no one else will have to know. Emily.

Emily (*goes to Mrs. Allen*): Yes, Ma'am.

(*Mrs. Allen whispers in her ear, and Emily nods her head happily.*)

Emily: Thank you, Ma'am. (*She goes back to her place.*)

Mrs. Allen: Don't thank me. You earned it. Frank.

Frank (*goes to Mrs. Allen*): Yes, Mrs. Allen.

Mrs. Allen (*whispers in his ear, and Frank looks happy*): I'm proud of you, Frank.

Frank: Thank you. (*Goes to his seat.*)

Mrs. Allen: Mary.

Mary (*goes to Mrs. Allen*): Here I am.

(*Mrs. Allen whispers in her ear.*)

Mary: You mean I passed?

Mrs. Allen: You certainly did. And you did better than I thought you would. Now, try to keep up the good work.

Mary: I will. (*Goes to her place.*)

Mrs. Allen: David.

David (*goes to Mrs. Allen*): I'm here.

(*Mrs. Allen whispers in his ear.*)

David: Does that mean I have to take social studies over again next year?

Mrs. Allen: That depends. I can give you some makeup work to do this summer. If you finish it and do a good job, you can move up with your classmates. Otherwise, you'll have to repeat the class.

David: You mean I have to study during the summer?

Mrs. Allen: Yes, if you don't want to repeat social studies.

David (*upset*): Oh, no! (*Goes back to his seat.*)

Emily: David got an *F,* David got an *F.* Ha, ha, ha, ha, ha.

Mrs. Allen: Quiet, Emily. What David got is none of your business.

Emily: Yes, Ma'am. But he flunked, didn't he?

Frank: Emily! Shut up.

Mrs. Allen: Frank, we don't use the words *shut up* in this class. Is that understood?

Frank: Yes, Mrs. Allen.

Mary: I'm sorry for you, David. But you can move up with us if you study hard this summer.

David: Now everyone knows I got an *F,* and everyone will think I'm stupid.

Mrs. Allen: You're not stupid, David. You just need to learn how to study. Now, run along, students. School is over for today.

(*Mrs. Allen exits left, students exit right.*)

(*Outside the school building.*)

(*David enters center, looking sad.*)

David: I hate school. I hate Emily, and I hate Mrs. Allen. I hate Frank too, and I even hate Mary. This whole place stinks.

(*Frank enters right.*)

Frank: Hi, David. Who are you talking to?

David: None of your business, Mr. Smarty-Pants-*A*-Student.

Frank: Excuse me! I was just trying to be friendly.

David: Why would an *A* student like you want to be friends with a dummy like me?

Frank: You're no dummy.

David: I am too. I got an *F,* didn't I?

Frank: Yeah, but you got it because you didn't study, not because you're dumb. However, it's pretty dumb not to study, so maybe you are dumb after all. (*Pause.*) Just kidding.

David (*halfheartedly*): Ha, ha. No, you're not. It was dumb not to study. But I hate studying. I'd rather do something fun like play basketball or computer games or watch a movie.

Frank: I know what you mean. But look at it this way. If you had studied harder for social studies, you wouldn't have all that makeup work to do this summer.

David: I have an idea!

Frank: What?

David: You like to play with me, don't you?

Frank: Yeah.

David: Then you could come over to my house this summer, and we could do my social studies together.

Frank: Nothing doing. That's your makeup work.

David: I thought you were my friend.

Frank: I am, but I'm not going to do your work for you.

David: Don't do it, just help me with it.

Frank: You got into this mess because you didn't study. Now you're trying to get out of it by making someone else do part of your work.

David: I knew you wouldn't understand.

Frank: David! Be reasonable.

David: Get lost.

Frank: Now you really are acting like a dummy. (*Exits right.*)

David: Now Frank doesn't like me anymore. It's all Mrs. Allen's fault. If she hadn't given me an *F,* I wouldn't be in this mess.

(*Mary enters left.*)

Mary: Hi, David.

David: Hi, yourself.

Mary: I felt sorry for you in class today. I know how awful it feels to get a bad grade.

David: At least you passed.

Mary: Yeah, I got a *B* on the test and a *C* for the class.

David: That sounds pretty good to me.

Mary: I don't like social studies much, but I really wanted to get a good grade. So I studied real hard for that last test.

David: I hate social studies too. How can you make yourself study for something you hate?

Mary: I told myself that even though I didn't like it, it was part of school, and I had to do it. So I made myself study it twenty minutes every day. Then I made it thirty minutes, and the more I tried, the better grades I got, and the more I began to like social studies.

David: You mean you actually like social studies now?

Mary: Well, not very much, but I like it better than I used to. Before, I got *D*s. Now I get *C*s. It feels good to get better grades.

David: I don't want to flunk.

Mary: You won't if you study this summer. It won't take a lot of time, maybe only half an hour a day. Then you can spend the rest of the time having fun.

David: I guess you're right. At least Mrs. Allen is giving me another chance to pass.

Mary: She's a pretty nice teacher.

David: I suppose so. Did you ever have to do makeup work during the summer?

Mary: Once. I decided after that I'd rather work harder during school and have my summers free.

David: I wish I'd done that.

Mary: It's not so hard. I lived through it, so you can too. See you in class tomorrow. It's the last day of school, you know, and Mrs. Allen will hand out awards.

David: I won't get an award, that's for sure. But I'm glad school is almost over.

(*Both exit center.*)

(*In class next day.*)

(*Mrs. Allen enters at left, and all four students enter at right. Mrs. Allen faces students, and students face audience.*)

Mrs. Allen: This is the last day of school. I want to wish all of you a good summer vacation. Do any of you have special plans?

Emily: I'm going to visit the nation's capital.

Mrs. Allen: Wonderful! You'll see a lot of things we've studied about in social studies.

Frank: I'm going to visit my grandparents in Canada.

Mrs. Allen: Good for you. You'll learn a lot about that country on your trip.

Mary: I'm not going anyplace this summer. But I plan to visit the library and read lots of books.

Mrs. Allen: That's an excellent idea.

David: I'm not going anywhere either. But I'm going to work real hard at my social studies makeup work, so I'll be ready for next year.

Mrs. Allen: Good for you, David. I'm proud of you.

David: You are?

Mrs. Allen: Yes. I hoped you would learn how to be a responsible student from this experience. And I think you're beginning to learn. Now, before we dismiss for the year, I have some awards to pass out. Emily, here is your award.

Emily: What's it for?

Mrs. Allen: For being a consistently good student.

Emily (*goes to Mrs. Allen for her award, then returns to her seat*): Thanks.

Mrs. Allen: Frank, I have an award for you. It's for having an excellent attitude about school.

Frank: Thanks. (*Gets award and returns to his place.*)

Mrs. Allen: Mary, your award is for trying the hardest.

Mary: An award? For me? Thanks! (*Gets award and sits down.*)

Mrs. Allen: David, I didn't know if I could give you this award until today. But you've proved to me that you deserve it.

David: I get an award? Me? The one who got an *F*?

Mrs. Allen: Yes. Your award is for having the most improved attitude.

David: Gee, thanks! (*Gets his award.*)

Mrs. Allen: Class dismissed. Have a wonderful summer. (*She exits left.*)

(*Students say the following lines at the same time.*)

Mary: Good-bye.

Frank: Summer. Whoopee!

Mary: Yay. School's out!

David: Yippee! School's over. And I got an award!

(*All exit right.*)

4
You Do Something You Know Is Wrong

Scripture: James 4:16-17; 1 John 1:9
Props: Bead necklace, charm bracelet, two dimes (All of these can be imaginary.)
Performance Time: 16 minutes
Characters: Carol, Janet, Beverly

(*In a wooded area.*)
(*Carol and Janet enter center stage.*)
Carol: This is so exciting! I've never had a secret clubhouse before.
Janet: The main word is *secret.* We can't tell anybody where the club is or that we have one.
Carol: I won't. I promise.
Janet: Let's seal our promise with a sign. We'll each hang something special to us on one of these bushes.
Carol: OK. I'll hang my special bead necklace on this bush. (*Takes off the necklace and hangs it on bush.*)
Janet: And I'll hang my charm bracelet. (*Takes it off and hangs it on bush.*) There. Now our promise is sealed. No one but you and I must ever know about the club.
Carol: This place is so special it ought to have a name.
Janet: That's a good idea.
Carol: The name should describe what our club looks like.
Janet: It's in the woods behind a cornfield. So maybe the words *woods* and *cornfield* could be in it.
Carol: And it's surrounded by tall bushes that you can crawl

through like tunnels. So maybe it could have the word *tunnels* in it.

Janet: Corn Wood Tunnels. How's that?

Carol: No. That's not special enough.

Janet: Then you think of one.

Carol: Tunnels in the Cornfield Woods. That has a nice ring to it. That will be our club's name.

Janet: Wait. I have another idea: Secret Tunnel Wood Club of the Cornfield.

Carol: That's too long.

Janet: Then you think of something better.

Carol: I'm trying to. Let's see: woods, tunnels, bushes, cornfield. How about Cornfield Tunnel Bushes?

Janet: Yuck. Is that all you can come up with?

Carol: It was just an idea. Don't get so upset. Anyway, what's so bad about Tunnels in the Cornfield Woods?

Janet: It stinks, that's what.

Carol: It does not.

Janet: Does too.

Carol: Does not.

Janet: Quit being so bossy.

Carol: I'm not bossy.

Janet: You are too.

Carol: We're never going to think of a name if we keep arguing.

Janet: That's the smartest thing you've said so far.

Carol: Maybe we shouldn't call it something that will help people find it.

Janet: You mean we shouldn't use words like *tunnel* and *bushes* and *woods* in the name?

Carol: Right. I've got an idea!

Janet: What?

Carol: Whoever comes up with the best name for the clubhouse gets to be president.

Janet: OK! What will the other person be?

Carol: Vice-president, of course.

Janet: Let's meet back here tomorrow. By then we should have some good names. (*Janet and Carol exit center.*)

(*On sidewalk later that day.*)
(*Carol enters right.*)
Carol: I really want to be president of the club. But I'll bet Janet won't like any of the names I come up with. What I need is a superduper name, something so good she can't turn up her nose at it.
(*Beverly enters left.*)
Beverly: Come along, Speedlebananas. That's a good boy.
Carol: Who are you talking to?
Beverly: My pet dog.
Carol: I don't see any dog.
Beverly: That's because he's not your pet. I'm the only one who can see him.
Carol: I get it. A make-believe pet.
Beverly: He's real, all right, aren't you, boy? Did you hear him yip?
Carol: No.
Beverly: He just told you he was real, and he's sorry you can't see him.
Carol: What's his name again?
Beverly: Speedlebananas.
Carol: What a weird name.
Beverly: I like it, and he likes it.
Carol: Where'd you come up with that name?
Beverly: I don't know. I just like to give things names. I call my spelling book Alpha Whopper-Dopper and my watch Ticky-Ricky Rooster.
Carol: Why do you give everything names?
Beverly: I just like to name things.
Carol: You do? Hmmmm. Did you ever name a club?
Beverly: No, I've never had one to name.
Carol: Would you like to name one?
Beverly: I sure would. That would be a real challenge.

Carol: If you had one, what would you name it?

Beverly: I don't know. I'd have to see it first and get the feel of the place.

Carol: Couldn't you just make up a name?

Beverly: Oh, no. Half the fun of naming something is to make the name match the personality of the thing I'm naming.

Carol: A club doesn't have a personality.

Beverly: Maybe not, but I'd still have to see it before I named it.

Carol: Forget it, then.

Beverly: Do you have a club?

Carol: None of your business.

Beverly: Tommy and Richard have a clubhouse. It's in the basement of the old vacant house across from the windmill on Dover Street. Oops! I forgot. I wasn't supposed to tell. You won't tell anyone, will you?

Carol: No. Who cares about their club, anyway? I've got my own.

Beverly: Aha! I knew it. You do have a club.

Carol: Well, yeah.

Beverly: Can I see it? Please? Please? I love clubs.

Carol: It's supposed to be a secret. Janet and I agreed not to tell anyone.

Beverly: But I'm not just anyone. I'm the one you asked to name your club, remember?

Carol: Will you give it a name?

Beverly: Sure.

Carol: Then I'll show it to you. I guess it won't matter if you see it because you'll come up with such a super name that I'll win our naming contest and be president. Then I can change the rules to say we can show just one other person the clubhouse.

Beverly: You mean if I come up with a great name, you'll be president?

Carol: Yeah. We're supposed to make up our own names, but I have to have a superspecial one or Janet won't like it.

Beverly: So, you're going to cheat.

Carol: I'm not sure I'd call it that. I'm just getting help.

Beverly: Sure.

Carol: Remember, if I show you the clubhouse, you mustn't tell anyone. Not Janet, your sister or brother or your friends. Not even your parents. OK?

Beverly: Of course, I can keep a secret.

Carol: Come on, then. (*Both exit right, then reenter left in the club.*)

Beverly: Wow, this is great! I love the way the bushes and trees form a sort of ceiling. No one could find this place unless they knew where to look. I love it!

Carol: What would you name it?

Beverly: That's easy. The name just pops right out all over this place.

Carol: Well, tell me.

Beverly: Ready for this?

Carol: Yes.

Beverly: Are you sure?

Carol: Of course, I'm sure. Now tell me what it is.

Beverly: I need a drumroll, this is so good.

Carol: The only drumroll you'll get is a thump on the head if you don't hurry up and tell me.

Beverly: OK, OK.

Carol: So tell me.

Beverly: Patience, please. Genius can't be rushed.

Carol: Brother!

Beverly: The name is (*pauses*) Bushel Dushel Palace.

Carol: Bushel Dushel Palace?

Beverly: Yeah. It's great, isn't it?

Carol: I guess so once you get used to it.

Beverly: I'm going to like coming to Bushel Dushel Palace.

Carol: But you can't!

Beverly: Why not?

Carol: Because it's a secret club, and only Janet and I belong to it.

Beverly: Can't I join?

Carol: No, it's supposed to be a secret. I wasn't supposed to tell anyone.

Beverly: But once you're president, you can change the rules. You said so yourself.

Carol: I'm not going to win the contest with a name like Bushel Dushel Palace.

Beverly: Don't you like that name?

Carol: I could have done better myself.

Beverly: Thanks a lot! I do you a favor, then you tell me you don't like it.

Carol: Get lost, Beverly.

Beverly: What's this?

Carol: My necklace.

Beverly: How come it's hanging on this bush?

Carol: Because. I hung it there to seal my promise.

Beverly: What promise?

Carol: That I'd never tell anyone about this place.

Beverly: You sure can't keep a promise very well.

Carol: Look who's talking. You told me about Tommy's and Richard's clubhouse.

Beverly: Maybe I'll tell about yours too.

Carol: You wouldn't!

Beverly: Not if you let me join.

Carol: I can't. I already told you that.

Beverly: Then your club won't be a secret much longer.

Carol: You can't tell! Here. (*Searches her pockets.*) I'll give you two dimes not to tell.

Beverly: Two dimes? Are you crazy? It will take a lot more than that to keep me quiet.

Carol: But that's all I have.

Beverly: What about this? (*Points to necklace on bush.*)

Carol: I can't give you that. I used it to seal my promise. It's part of the club.

Beverly: I think I'll tell Mary about your club first. She'll tell her brother, Charlie. Then he and his friends will come over here and tear . . .

Carol: No! Here, you can have the necklace.

Beverly: And the bracelet.

Carol (*wails*): But, Beverly, that's not mine. It belongs to Janet.

Beverly: Then I'm going straight to Mary.

Carol: All right, take the bracelet too. But that's all I have. (*Beverly takes the bracelet.*)

Beverly: Give me your dimes, and my lips are sealed forever.

Carol (*angrily*): Here. You may make up good names for some things, but you sure aren't a very nice person.

Beverly: Look, Miss Not-So-Good-Yourself. You're the one who came to me for help because you wanted to cheat on the naming contest. And you're the one who told me about the club when you promised not to.

Carol: Get out of here, Beverly. I don't ever want to see you again.

Beverly (*in a snooty tone*): Bye. (*Beverly exits left.*)

Carol: Now look what I've done! Beverly will tell, I just know it. Why did I ever ask her to help me name this place? I should have let Janet win the naming contest and be president of the club. Now we might not even have a secret club for anyone to be president of.

(*Janet enters right.*)

Janet: Hi, Carol. Why are you looking so sad?

Carol: Uh, hi, Janet. I'm sad because . . . because, uh, because . . . we've been robbed. That's it. Robbed.

Janet: Robbed?

Carol: Yeah. Isn't it awful? Someone stole our jewelry.

Janet: My bracelet. It's gone!

Carol: So's my necklace.

Janet: That was a special bracelet. My grandma and lots of other relatives gave me charms for it. One used to be my great-grandmother's. My mom will kill me if she finds out it's gone.

Carol: Well, how do you think I feel? My necklace is gone too.

Janet: You know what this means?

Carol: What?

Janet: It means someone knows about our secret club.

Carol: That's awful.

Janet: It's terrible, just terrible. Now we'll have to find a new one.

Carol: You're right. Let's start looking right away.

Janet: Maybe we should forget about another club until we find our jewelry.

Carol: We'll never find it.

Janet: We'll have to be good detectives. The first clue should be looking for footprints.

Carol: Footprints? In this place? There are too many leaves and twigs and stuff for footprints.

Janet: You're right. Then we'll just have to watch and see if anyone wears our jewelry.

Carol: Uh, yeah, I guess so. If someone does, what do we do?

Janet: Tell her to give it back.

Carol: Oh, sure. She'll say it's hers.

Janet: Maybe, but I can prove the charm bracelet belongs to me. One charm has my name on it, another has my great-grandmother's name. And, besides, my mom and dad will be able to identify it.

Carol: Oh.

Janet: Come on, let's start looking.

Carol (*halfheartedly*): OK. (*They exit right.*)

(*On the sidewalk the next day.*)

(*Beverly enters left, Janet enters right. Janet sees Beverly wearing her bracelet and Carol's necklace and runs up to her.*)

Janet: So you're the crook!

Beverly: I beg your pardon.

Janet: That's my bracelet you're wearing, thief. Give it here.

Beverly: Don't call me a thief.

Janet: I will because that's what you are. Now give me that bracelet.

Beverly: No. It belonged to my dear departed great-grandmother.

Janet: Now you're a liar too. If you don't give it to me now, I'll tell the teacher, the principal, your parents, your Sunday School teacher, and . . . and your neighbors and . . . and . . . and the president of the United States!

Beverly: You do, and I'll tell where your club is.

Janet: Who cares? We're going to move it anyway now that you
    know. Hey, how did you find out about it?

Beverly: Your blabbermouth friend, Carol, told me.

Janet: Carol? I don't believe it.

Beverly: How do you think I got your bracelet?

Janet: You stole it.

Beverly: No, I didn't. Carol gave it to me so I wouldn't tell
    anyone about your club.

Janet: Why, that little two-timing sneak.

Beverly: She gave me her necklace and twenty cents too.

Janet: I can't believe it! I just can't believe it.

Beverly: It's true.

Janet: You're no better than she is, you blackmailer. I'm going to
    tell the teacher what you did.

Beverly: No need for that. I'll give you back your bracelet. Here.
    (*Hands Janet the bracelet.*)

Janet: And Carol's necklace.

Beverly: Oh, all right! Here. (*Beverly hands her the necklace.*)

Janet: And the twenty cents?

Beverly: Can't do that.

Janet: Why not?

Beverly: I already spent it.

Janet: Get out of here, and if you ever do anything to Carol or
    me again, I'll tell the teacher you blackmailed Carol.

Beverly: All right, all right, I'm going. (*She exits left.*)

(*Carol enters right.*)

Carol: I've looked all over and haven't found a sign of our jewel-
    ry.

Janet: I had better luck. Look! (*Holds up the jewelry.*)

Carol: My necklace! And your bracelet!

Janet: Sorry I couldn't get your twenty cents back.

Carol: That's OK. I mean, uh, er, twenty cents? What twenty
    cents?

Janet: Quit acting so innocent, Carol. I know all about it. Beverly
    told me everything.

Carol: Oh.

Janet: I can't believe you told her about our club and gave her my bracelet.

Carol: I know it was wrong.

Janet: And then you had the gall to tell me we'd been robbed.

Carol: I was afraid you'd hate me if you found out what I'd done.

Janet: I don't hate you. But I feel betrayed. I thought you were my friend.

Carol: I am.

Janet: Then why did you tell Beverly about the club?

Carol: Because she's so good at naming things I wanted her to think of a name for our club.

Janet: Didn't you trust yourself to come up with a good name?

Carol: I wanted a supergood name so, so, well, so I could be president.

Janet (*astonished*): You mean you told about our club just so you could win the naming contest and be president?

Carol: Yes. I know it was wrong. I don't know why I thought it was so important to be president.

Janet: I do. You like to be in charge all the time.

Carol: No, I don't.

Janet: Yes, you do, and it makes me sick.

Carol: Please, Janet, don't be mad at me. I feel bad enough.

Janet: Tell me, Miss Bossy Face, what did she name the club?

Carol: The Bushel Dushel Palace.

Janet: Bushel Dushel Palace? That's the most awful name I ever heard.

Carol: I know. I guess she doesn't always come up with good names. I should have trusted myself to come up with a good name.

Janet: You sure should have. I had a much better name picked out than Beverly's.

Carol: What?

Janet: The Two-Girl-Gang Hideout.

Carol: Yuck.

Janet: You don't like it?

Carol: No. It's worse than Bushel Dushel Palace.

Janet: You never like anything I pick. You always want your name, your idea, your everything. I'm sick of you.

Carol: I always want my own everything? Me? You've got that turned around, Miss Always-Wants-Her-Own-Way.

Janet: You've got a lot of nerve calling me names after what you did.

Carol: You're right. I'll try to do better. Honest! Please don't stop being my friend.

Janet: Ah, how could I stop being your friend? You make life interesting. I never know what you're going to do next. (*Pauses.*) I guess we don't have to worry about a name now that we don't have a clubhouse anymore.

Carol: It was all my fault. I really am sorry.

Janet: You ought to be. You broke a promise, you tried to cheat on the naming contest, you gave away something that wasn't yours, and you lied. You're a real mess.

Carol: I said I was sorry, several times.

Janet: I know. And I forgive you. It may be a while, though, before I can trust you again.

Carol: I want you to trust me.

Janet: Trust is something you have to earn.

Carol: You just watch. I'll prove I'm trustworthy.

Janet: At least something good came out of all this.

Carol: What?

Janet: We got our jewelry back.

Carol: Yeah.

Janet: Come on, let's get a snack at my house. Someday maybe we can look for another clubhouse.

(*Both exit center.*)

5
You Tell a Lie

Scripture: Proverbs 19:5
Props: Two pinewood derby cars (They can be imaginary.)
Performance Time: 14 minutes
Characters: Jim, Mark, Eric, Mr. Winters, Mr. Baldwin, Sam, Henry

(*In front of Mark's house.*)
(*Jim and Mark enter center stage.*)
Jim: Are you going to enter the pinewood derby, Mark?
Mark: I sure am. I'm putting the finishing touches on my car now. I think it will be really fast.
Jim: Faster than Eric's?
Mark: I don't know. I haven't seen his car yet.
Jim: It's sleek. It has a neat sloped front to cut down on wind resistance. He painted it red with a black zigzag stripe along the sides.
Mark: Are you sure he made it and painted it?
Jim: He said he did.
Mark: Yeah? Well, it wouldn't surprise me if he bought that car.
Jim: What makes you think so?
Mark: I don't know. It just sounds too sharp for Eric to have made by himself.
Jim: If he didn't make it, he can't be in the race. You know the rules. We have to make our own cars—from scratch.
Mark: I know. I'll bet Eric bought his car last year too. That's probably how he won.

Jim: Are you accusing him of cheating?

Mark: No, I'm just thinking out loud.

Jim: You'd better not think out loud in front of anyone else unless you have proof Eric really cheated.

Mark: Yeah, yeah. How's your car coming?

Jim: It's all done. It goes pretty fast, but I don't think it's fast enough to beat you or Eric. You came in second behind Eric last year, didn't you?

Mark: Yeah, and the year before that, and the year before that. I have a bunch of second-place trophies.

Jim: Maybe this year you'll win.

Mark: I hope so. That first-place trophy is really neat.

Jim: And the first-place winner gets five free movie passes and a free dinner for his whole family at a fancy restaurant.

Mark: I sure would like to win.

Jim: See you later. I've got to get home.

(*Jim and Mark exit center.*)

(*At Eric's house.*)

(*Eric and his dad, Mr. Winters, enter right.*)

Eric: I've checked it all out, Dad, and I think my car's as good as it can be.

Mr. Winters: It's a beauty, Son. You're getting very good at making cars. I'm proud of you.

Eric: Thanks, Dad, but you helped me some with the painting.

Mr. Winters: You're giving me more credit than I deserve. All I did was suggest which colors to use so you wouldn't get them mixed up.

Eric: I hate not being able to tell colors apart.

Mr. Winters: Your granddad was color blind too, and he did just fine. He lived a long, happy life.

Eric: You always say that.

Mr. Winters: It's true. And look at you. You built that car all by yourself. I know because I watched you do it right from the start. And it's beautiful.

Eric: It does look pretty nice, doesn't it? Think I'll win again this year?

Mr. Winters: I think you have a good chance, Son. But if you don't, you'll have fun trying anyway.

Eric: That's true. I love pinewood derbies.

(*Mr. Winters and Eric exit right.*)

(*At Mr. Baldwin's house.*)

(*Enter Mr. Baldwin center. Mark enters left.*)

Mr. Baldwin: Hi, Mark, what brings you to my house?

Mark: Hi, Mr. Baldwin. You're in charge of the pinewood derby tomorrow, aren't you?

Mr. Baldwin: Yep.

Mark: I brought my car over to show you. (*Holds it up.*) What do you think?

Mr. Baldwin: It's very nice. I see you put a lot of work into it.

Mark: Thanks. I think it's important to do your best on everything, even making cars for the pinewood derby. Don't you?

Mr. Baldwin: You bet. I'm glad to see you're learning how to be responsible.

Mark: I feel sorry for people who don't have the fun of making their derby cars from scratch.

Mr. Baldwin: What do you mean? Everyone makes their cars from scratch for the derby.

Mark: Er, of course, they do.

Mr. Baldwin: Do you know someone who isn't making his car from scratch?

Mark: Er, uh, no. No, I don't.

Mr. Baldwin: If you know someone is breaking the rules and don't tell me, then you're just as bad as they are because you're helping them cheat.

Mark: Well, uh . . .

Mr. Baldwin: Go on, Son.

Mark: Well, see, I think . . . uh, I have a feeling Eric bought his car.

Mr. Baldwin: Eric Winters?

Mark: Yeah.

Mr. Baldwin: But he won last year. He's been entering cars in the derby for years, and he's made them every year. He gets better each year too. Why would he buy a car this time?

Mark: I don't know.

Mr. Baldwin: Are you sure he bought it?

Mark: Well, uh, I'm pretty sure.

Mr. Baldwin: Thanks for telling me, Mark. I know you didn't want to tell on your friend. But if he's cheating, you did the right thing.

Mark: If you say so. But, please, don't tell anyone I said anything to you about it.

Mr. Baldwin: Don't worry. Your secret is safe with me.

(*Mr. Baldwin exits center. Mark exits right.*)

(*In front of Mark's house.*)
(*Mark enters center. Jim enters left.*)

Jim: You look pleased with yourself. What's up?

Mark: I have a feeling I might win the pinewood derby this year.

Jim: Think you can beat Eric? He's beaten you every year for as long as I can remember.

Mark: I know, but I have a special feeling about this race. I really think I'm going to win.

Jim: Well, good luck.

Mark: What brings you over here?

Jim: Oh! I almost forgot. Mr. Baldwin has called a meeting of all the racers at his house. We're supposed to be there in fifteen minutes.

Mark: Hmmm. This is the first time he's ever called a meeting the day before the race.

Jim: Maybe he wants to go over all the rules again.

Mark: Maybe. See you there.

(*Jim and Mark exit left.*)

(*At Mr. Baldwin's house.*)
(*Mr. Baldwin enters center. Eric, Mark, and Jim enter left.*)

Eric: Hi, Mr. Baldwin. Jim told me you called a meeting.

Mr. Baldwin: Yes. I'm talking to a few of you at a time.

Jim: Why, Sir?

Mr. Baldwin: I want to stress one of the rules.

Eric: But we know all the rules.

Mr. Baldwin: The rule I want to stress is the one we all decided to follow several years ago. It has to do with the cars themselves. Does anyone know which rule I'm talking about?

Jim: I'm not sure.

Eric: Me, neither.

Mark: Tell us.

Mr. Baldwin: Several years ago we decided that everyone in the pinewood derby would make their own cars. Remember that rule?

Jim, Eric, and Mark: Yes.

Mr. Baldwin: We made that rule because we thought it would teach all of you to be more creative and to learn how wind and other factors affect the speed of your car.

Eric: We know that, Mr. Baldwin.

Mr. Baldwin: People are supposed to make the cars by themselves and not buy them ready-made. Do you all remember?

Jim, Mark, and Eric: Yes.

Mr. Baldwin: It has come to my attention that someone bought his car for tomorrow's race.

Eric: He did?

Jim: No kidding?

Mark: I made mine.

Mr. Baldwin: What about you, Jim?

Jim: I made mine.

Eric: I made mine too.

Mr. Baldwin: I see. All right. The meeting's over. Eric, would you mind staying for a while?

Eric: No, I don't mind. See you later, guys.

(*Mark and Jim exit left.*)

Mr. Baldwin: I'm going to ask you one more time, Eric. Did you make your car?

Eric: Yes, all by myself.

Mr. Baldwin: Are you sure?

Eric: Yes! If you don't believe me, ask my dad. He saw me make it.

Mr. Baldwin: I think that's a good idea. I need to have a look at your car too.

Eric: Why? Do you think I cheated? I've raced in the pinewood derby for years. I've never broken the rules.

Mr. Baldwin: I know, Eric. But someone told me he thought you bought your car, and I have to find out whether you broke the rule.

Eric: Then someone's lying to you.

Mr. Baldwin: We'll find out. This evening I'll be over to take a look at your car and talk to your dad.

Eric: Good! Then you'll know I'm telling the truth.

(*Eric exits left. Mr. Baldwin exits center.*)

(*On the sidewalk.*)

(*Mark and Jim enter center.*)

Jim: That's a strange thing Mr. Baldwin just did. All that talk about making your own car. Why does he think someone cheated?

Mark: Gee, I don't know.

Jim: Wait a minute. You told me you thought Eric bought his car.

Mark: Yeah, but I don't know for sure.

Jim: What if someone else actually saw him buy it and told Mr. Baldwin? That would explain why he told Eric to stay and why he let us leave.

Mark: Maybe.

Jim: If Eric bought his car, you know what that means? He'll be disqualified, and you might win the derby.

Mark: You're right.

Jim: I just can't imagine Eric buying his car. He's really good at making them.

Mark: Maybe he got too busy this year.

Jim: Maybe. Well, I'll see you later.

(*Jim exits center. Sam enters right.*)

Sam: Hey, Mark, did you get called to Mr. Baldwin's house?

Mark: Yeah.

Sam: What did he tell you?

Mark: He said it had come to his attention that someone might have bought his derby car instead of making it.

Sam: That's what he told us too. Who would do something like that?

Mark: Mr. Baldwin thinks it might have been Eric.

Sam: No kidding! Maybe he's been buying his cars every year. No wonder he always wins. Boy, what a jerk! And I thought he was such a neat guy.

(*Mark exits center. Henry enters right.*)

Sam: Henry, guess what?

Henry: What?

Sam: That rat Eric bought his own car for the derby this year.

Henry: So he's the one! I never would have guessed it was him.

Sam: That's probably how he won all these years.

Henry: What a cheat! Wait till I tell the rest of the guys. They'll never believe it.

Sam: Someone ought to knock some sense into Eric's head. Mr. Baldwin might have called off the whole derby if he hadn't found out who the cheater was.

Henry: That really would have been awful.

(*Eric enters left.*)

Eric: Hi, Sam and Henry.

Sam: Get lost, cheater!

Henry: Yeah, get lost, you car buyer!

Eric: Hey, I didn't buy my car. What is this, anyway? A lynch mob?

Sam: No, just two guys who finally know the truth about you.

Henry: You've been cheating all these years, and it finally caught up with you.

Eric: That's not true.

Sam: Save your breath. We know the truth.

Henry: I hope they disqualify you from every derby you ever try
to enter.

Eric: But . . .

(*Sam and Henry exit center.*)

Eric: How did this happen? I don't understand. Everyone thinks
I cheated. (*Eric exits left.*)

(*At Eric's house.*)

(*Mr. Baldwin enters right.*)

Mr. Baldwin: Knock, knock.

(*Mr. Winters enters left.*)

Mr. Winters: Hi. Eric told me you were coming.

Mr. Baldwin: Yes, I'd like to see Eric's car.

Mr. Winters: Sure. (*Calls out.*) Eric, bring your car and come
here.

(*Eric enters left.*)

Eric: Hi, Mr. Baldwin. Here's my car. I made it. Honest!

Mr. Baldwin (*looks carefully at car*): This is very well made, Eric,
better made than most cars I've seen for sale in the store.

Eric: See the way the front slopes to keep the wind resistance
down?

Mr. Baldwin: Yes.

Eric: I did a lot of math to figure out just what the slant should
be.

Mr. Winters: That's true. He filled several sheets with calcula-
tions before he started building his car.

Mr. Baldwin: Did you see Eric build it?

Mr. Winters: I sure did. He worked hard on it.

Mr. Baldwin: This paint job is so good, it looks professional.
Forgive me, but it's hard to believe a child could have done
this.

Eric: But I did. Tell him, Dad. You picked out the paint for me.

Mr. Baldwin: You're not supposed to get that kind of help from
your dad, Eric.

Eric: But . . .

Mr. Winters: What he's trying to say is that he's color blind. It runs in the family. My father was color blind too. I told him what colors I thought would go well together, and from the suggestions I gave him he picked two colors. Then he did all the painting himself.

Mr. Baldwin: Do you have the cans of paint in the house?

Mr. Winters: Yes, we still have them. You're welcome to look at them. They'll prove Eric didn't buy the car.

Eric: Come, we'll show you. (*All three exit left, then return.*)

Mr. Baldwin: I believe you, Eric. All the evidence is there. You made the car all right. Someone gave me false information. I apologize.

Mr. Winters: It's all right. You're just doing your job.

Eric: We forgive you, Mr. Baldwin. See you at the race tomorrow. (*Eric and Mr. Winters exit center. Mr. Baldwin exits right.*)

(*At Mark's house.*)
(*Mr. Baldwin enters right.*)
Mr. Baldwin: Knock, knock.
(*Mark enters left.*)
Mark: Come in.

Mr. Baldwin: Mark, why did you tell me Eric bought his car?

Mark: Because, er, I, well, uh, that is, I told you I *thought* he did.

Mr. Baldwin: Why did you tell me that?

Mark: Uh, because, er, because I know how important it is to be honest and do your best. And you urged me to tell.

Mr. Baldwin: But you weren't honest with me, were you?

Mark (meekly): No, Sir.

Mr. Baldwin: You knew Eric didn't cheat, but you made me believe he did. Do you know what it's called when someone tells you something that isn't true?

Mark: A lie.

Mr. Baldwin: That's right. You lied to me. And I have a feeling I know why.

Mark: But I thought it was true.

Mr. Baldwin: You wanted me to think Eric cheated so I'd disqualify him from the race. Then you'd have a chance to win. Am I right?

Mark: Uh, well, sort of.

Mr. Baldwin: There's no sort of about it. You deliberately lied to get Eric disqualified. That's an awful thing to do.

Mark: Yes, Sir. I'll never do it again. I promise. Now Eric and I can compete fair and square tomorrow.

Mr. Baldwin: You won't be competing tomorrow.

Mark: Mr. Baldwin, please. I've got to compete.

Mr. Baldwin: I'm disqualifying you from the race. Anyone who lies about a competitor to give himself a better chance to win doesn't deserve to race in the derby.

Mark: I said I was sorry.

Mr. Baldwin: And I'm sorry I believed you when you came to me with that story about Eric. You set me up. I should have known Eric would never do something like that.

Mark: Please let me compete, Mr. Baldwin. Please.

Mr. Baldwin: No, Mark. You have to pay the consequences for what you've done. Part of your punishment will be going to everyone you told the lie to and telling them the truth.

Mark: But I can't. That's too humiliating.

Mr. Baldwin: Don't you think Eric felt humiliated when everyone accused him of cheating?

Mark: I suppose.

Mr. Baldwin: If you don't apologize to everyone you lied to, you'll never compete in another derby as long as I'm in charge. And you'll apologize to Eric too.

Mark: Yes, Sir.

(*Mark exits left. Mr. Baldwin exits right.*)

(*In front of Eric's house.*)

(*Mark enters left.*)

Mark: I'm so tired. I talked to Jim and Sam and everyone else I told that lie to. The only person left is Eric. He's going to be the hardest one to face. I might as well get it over with. Knock, knock.

(*Eric enters right.*)

Eric: Mark, come in.

Mark: I came to apologize.

Eric: For what?

Mark: For telling everyone you bought your derby car.

Eric: So you're the one.

Mark: I'm sorry.

Eric: Everyone was mad at me. It was awful. Mr. Baldwin came over here and made me prove I made my own car. It's a good thing you didn't come here any sooner. I was really mad for a while.

Mark: I shouldn't have told everyone you bought the car.

Eric: Why did you tell that lie?

Mark: Because . . . because I wanted to win.

Eric: Winning meant so much to you that you were willing to lie?

Mark: It was stupid, I know.

Eric: Yes, it was. But I forgive you.

Mark: You do?

Eric: Yeah.

Mark: Why? I did something pretty awful to you.

Eric: Yes, you did. But people did things a lot worse to Jesus, and He forgave them. Besides, it won't do me any good to stay mad at you. I'd just feel angry, and I wouldn't have any fun.

Mark: I never thought of it that way.

Eric: On top of that, you're a pretty good car racer. And anyone who races cars in derbies can't be all bad.

Mark: Thanks, Eric. But I won't be in the race tomorrow.

Eric: You won't?

Mark: No. I've been disqualified. It's my punishment for lying.

Eric: That's too bad.

Mark: I was mad about it at first. But now I think Mr. Baldwin was right not to let me race.

Eric: I think he was too. But next year we can race our cars against each other.

Mark: I'll look forward to that.

Eric: Come on. I'll show you my car. It's real neat.

Mark: OK.

(*Both exit center.*)

6
You See Someone Do Something Wrong

Scripture: 1 Thessalonians 5:14
Props: One pearl necklace, three colorful necklaces, one blue necklace
Performance Time: 8 minutes
Characters: Mary, Rose, Danny, woman cashier

(*In a store*)
(*Mary and Rose enter center.*)
Mary: Look at everything in this store! There are so many things I'll have a hard time choosing just one for Mom's birthday.
Rose: Why choose just one thing?
Mary: Because I only have two dollars.
Rose: Don't let a little thing like that bother you.
Mary: What do you mean?
Rose: You wait and see.
Mary: Let's walk up the jewelry aisle. Maybe I can find a nice necklace for Mom.
(*Mary and Rose walk toward left pretending to look at necklaces and bracelets. While they look, Rose puts things in her pocket when she thinks no one is looking. Mary doesn't notice what Rose is doing.*)
Mary: This is a pretty blue necklace, and it's only one dollar and seventy-five cents. It will look nice with Mom's good white blouse.
Rose: Let's buy it quick and get out of here.
Mary: You're in a hurry all of a sudden.

Rose: Yeah, well, like I always say, never stay in one spot longer than you have to.

Mary: I've never heard you say that before.

Rose: How about if I wait outside while you buy the necklace?

Mary: OK. I'll be just a minute.

(*Rose exits right. Woman cashier enters left.*)

Cashier: Hi, can I help you?

Mary: Yes. I'd like to buy this necklace. It's for my Mom. Her birthday is tomorrow.

Cashier: How nice of you. I have a daughter about your age. If she bought me a necklace for my birthday, it would make me feel real good.

Mary: I hope my mom feels the same way. Here's the money for the necklace. I earned it by helping Dad clean out the garage.

Cashier: Good for you. Here's your change and your necklace.

Mary: Thanks. Bye.

(*Mary exits right, cashier exits left.*)

(*At Rose's house.*)

(*Mary and Rose enter right.*)

Mary: Thanks for letting me come over to your house and wrap my present for Mom. Now she won't know about her present until it's her birthday.

Rose: You're welcome.

Mary: I wish you could have found something at the store too. It's no fun to shop and come home empty-handed.

Rose: I did find something.

Mary: I didn't think you had time to go through the checkout line.

Rose: Who needs a checkout line?

Mary: That's the only way you can buy things.

Rose: Who said anything about buying?

Mary: You mean you took something without paying for it?

Rose: Sure. It's fun. Let me show you something. (*She pulls out a string of pearls.*) See these?

Mary (*gasps*): Rose! Those were marked twenty dollars!

Rose: I know. Wouldn't you like to give them to your mom? They're prettier than that blue necklace you bought.

Mary: I can't take them.

Rose: Why not? They're a gift.

Mary: You stole them. I can't give Mom something that I didn't get fair and square.

Rose: Don't be silly. The store has dozens more just like it. They won't miss this one.

Mary: Don't you know the Ten Commandments?

Rose: Sure.

Mary: Then you know one of the Commandments says, "Thou shalt not steal."

Rose: Don't be such a goody-two-shoes. That was written for the Israelites, not for me. I can steal if I want to.

Mary: The Ten Commandments are for everyone.

Rose: If God didn't want me to steal, He'd have struck me down long ago because I've stolen lots of things. Look, I got four necklaces today. (*She holds up three glittery necklaces along with the pearl necklace.*)

Mary: You took all those?

Rose: Sure. It was easy.

Mary: Rose, you're a thief!

Rose: No, I'm not. I just take a few things every once in a while. Thieves steal for a living.

Mary: You're a thief if you steal even a little.

Rose: I thought you were my friend. I'm not so sure now that you're calling me names.

Mary: I feel sorry for you. Someday you're going to get in a lot of trouble if you don't quit shoplifting.

Rose: I won't get caught. I'm real good at it. My cousin Charlie taught me.

Mary: Does he live around here?

Rose: Not anymore. He got busted for stealing a car, and he's in prison.

Mary: That's where you'll end up if you don't quit taking things that don't belong to you.

Rose: Cut the lecture, OK?

Mary: I'm going home.

Rose: Tell your mom happy birthday. Are you sure you don't want to give her the pearl necklace?

Mary: You still don't understand, do you? (*Mary exits left.*)

Rose: Poor Mary. She doesn't know what she's missing. She could have so many nice things if only she'd let me teach her a few tricks. (*Rose exits right.*)

(*At Mary's house.*)

(*Mary enters left.*)

Mary: What am I going to do? Rose took those necklaces, and I know about it. If I don't report what she did, doesn't that make me sort of guilty too? But if I report it, she'll hate me forever. (*Sighs.*) I wish life weren't so complicated.

(*Danny enters right.*)

Danny: Hi, Sis. What's wrong?

Mary: Nothing.

Danny: Don't try to fool me. I'm your big brother, remember? I can tell when something's bothering you.

Mary: I don't know if I should talk about it.

Danny: Talking about it might help.

Mary: But if I talk about it, I'll be snitching on a friend.

Danny: Did your friend do something wrong?

Mary: Yeah, and I don't know if I should report her.

Danny: What did she do?

Mary: She shoplifted four necklaces.

Danny: Uh-oh! That's serious.

Mary: What do you think I should do?

Danny: I don't know, but if I were the store owner, I sure would want those necklaces back.

Mary: Maybe I should steal them from Rose and take them back to the store myself. No, then I'd be stealing, and the store owner would think I took them in the first place.

Danny: Scratch plan A. What's plan B?

Mary: There isn't any plan B. I don't know what to do.

Danny: Do you think you'd be helping your friend if you turned her in?

Mary: She wouldn't think so, but maybe it would stop her from getting into bigger trouble later on.

Danny: That sounds like a pretty good reason for reporting her.

Mary: But who should I report her to? If I tell the store owner, she'll get in real big trouble.

Danny: Probably.

Mary: If I tell her parents, she might get a whipping.

Danny: Yeah.

Mary: But a whipping is better than being thrown in jail.

Danny: Probably.

Mary: But she might stop being my friend if she finds out I snitched on her.

Danny: Maybe.

Mary: Danny! You're supposed to be helping me. All you're doing is saying "yeah," "probably," and "maybe."

Danny: That's because it's your problem, and you have to decide what to do.

Mary: Oooh! I hate it when you say that.

Danny: So what are you going to do?

Mary: Maybe I'll tell Rose's parents. They know her better than anyone else. They'll probably know how to handle her better than the store owner or the police.

Danny: You're pretty smart for a little sister.

Mary: Think I'm doing the right thing?

Danny: I guess we'll find out.

Mary: Oooh! I hate it when you say things like that! Why don't you just say yes or no?

Danny: So you can't blame me if your plan backfires.

Mary: Oh, you!

Danny: And so you'll get smarter and more grown up by making your own decisions.

Mary: More grown up, huh?

Danny: And almost as smart as me.

Mary: You conceited brat! I'll show you how well I can hit you over the head.

Danny: You'll have to catch me first.

(*Mary chases Danny off stage left.*)

(*Outside Rose's house.*)

(*Mary and Rose enter right.*)

Mary: Hi, Rose. Can you come out and play?

Rose: No. I've been grounded for one month.

Mary: How come?

Rose: You know how come.

Mary: No, I don't.

Rose: Some little snitch told my parents about the necklaces I stole.

Mary: Oh.

Rose: And that little snitch was you!

Mary: How'd you find out?

Rose: You're the only one who knew about the necklaces. It had to be you.

Mary: I was just trying to keep you from getting into bigger trouble when you get older. If you quit shoplifting now, you can break the bad habit you have before you end up in jail.

Rose: OK, little Miss Preacher.

Mary: Do you hate me?

Rose: Yes.

Mary: Then I'll go. You don't want someone you hate hanging around.

Rose: Wait. I didn't mean it. I don't really hate you.

Mary: You don't?

Rose: Nah. You wouldn't have snitched on me if you didn't care about me.

Mary: You're right about that.

Rose: Mom and Dad bought those necklaces I took. They used my allowance money for the next year to pay for them. So I'll be pretty poor for a while.

Mary: They're punishing you kind of hard.

Rose: Know what else they did?

Mary: What?

Rose: They bought me some beads so I can make my own neck-laces to sell in a little gift shop my aunt runs downtown. I have to be at my little section of the store for one hour every day after school.

Mary: Wow, that sounds neat.

Rose: They had a sneaky reason for doing it.

Mary: What was that?

Rose: They want me to know what it feels like to be a merchant and have people shoplift from me.

Mary: Do people shoplift from your aunt's store?

Rose: All the time. My aunt had to raise all her prices to help pay for the losses.

Mary: That's too bad.

Rose: I know all the tricks of the trade. If someone tries to lift my necklaces, I'll really plaster them.

Mary: You're lucky to have such smart parents.

Rose: I guess they know what they're doing. And I guess you do too. I'm lucky to have you for a friend.

Mary: Thanks. I'm sure glad you're not mad at me.

Rose: I'm not mad, but I won't forget what you did—until you come to the store and get a necklace from me.

Mary: Make me a pretty one, and I'll buy it as soon as I have the money.

Rose: I'll give it to you for being such a good friend. It will be my birthday present to you.

Mary: Thanks, friend!

(*Both exit center.*)

7
You're Too Scared to Witness for Jesus

Scripture: Matthew 28:19-20
Props: None
Performance Time: 7 minutes
Characters: James, Helen, Charles, Grace

(*At James and Helen's house.*)

James (*enters center*): Wow! Helen, come quick! You've got to see this.

Helen (*enters right*): See what?

James: Look what's coming off that moving van.

Helen: Good grief! That furniture must be expensive. It looks so big and fluffy.

James: I've never seen such fancy stuff.

Helen: It looks like we're going to have rich neighbors.

James: Rich neighbors with kids. See all those toys?

Helen: Yeah, dolls and trucks and a bunch of other stuff.

James: I hope the boy's my age.

Helen: And I hope the girl's my age.

James: Hey, look, here comes a fancy van into the driveway.

Helen: A lady, a man, a girl, and a boy are getting out.

James: Yay! They look about our ages.

Helen: But they look so sophisticated. Look at their fancy clothes and the royal way they walk. I'll bet they won't want to play with us. We're just ordinary people.

James: Come on, let's introduce ourselves and ask if we can help.

Helen: OK. (*James and Helen exit right.*)

(*In Charles and Grace's front yard.*)
(*James and Helen enter right. Grace and Charles enter left.*)
James: Hi, we're your neighbors. We came to welcome you.
Helen: He's James, and I'm Helen. We're glad you're here.
Charles: Thank you so much.
Grace: How kind of you to come.
James: Your parents must have already gone inside.
Grace: They're not our parents.
Helen: They're not?
Grace: No. They're servants. Mother and Father will come later
   after they finish their business in the city.
Charles: Mother runs a modeling agency, and Father heads a
   large corporation. They sent us ahead with the servants, so
   we could start enjoying our month's vacation by the lake.
Grace: I can hardly wait to go swimming.
Helen: We can show you all the best places. We live here year
   round, so we know everything about this place.
Grace: Native folk. How quaint!
James: When you get unpacked, come on over, and we'll show
   you around.
Charles: Thanks. That would be lovely.
(*James and Helen exit right. Charles and Grace exit left.*)

(*At the home of James and Helen.*)
(*James and Helen enter right.*)
Helen: How quaint! What did she mean by that?
James: It's just big-city sophisticated talk.
Helen: They're going to think we're real country bumpkins.
James: So what? Country bumpkins can teach big-city snobs a
   trick or two.
Helen: Do you think they'll be fun to play with?
James: I hope so.
Helen: Maybe we should introduce them to some of our friends
   so they'll start to feel at home.
James: Good idea.

Helen: Let's invite them to church on Sunday. Lots of kids in our
    Sunday School class are their age.
James: Think they'd go?
Helen: We'll find out soon. Here they come now.
(*Charles and Grace enter left.*)
Charles: We're ready to go swimming.
Grace: Will you show us the best spot?
James: Sure. Follow us.
(*All four exit right.*)

(*At edge of lake.*)
(*All four enter right.*)
James: Here you are. It has a nice beach and gets deeper gradually
    with a great view of the lake bottom if you have goggles.
Charles: Wonderful. Thanks so much.
Helen: Uh, we know you're new around here, so we thought you
    might like to go to church with us and meet more of the kids
    in Sunday School.
Grace: Church? Goodness, no. We haven't been to church for
    ages.
Charles: Not since Great-Grandma died, God rest her soul.
Grace: But thanks for the invitation. I told you they were delight-
    fully quaint, Charles.
Charles: Thanks for showing us this good swimming spot.
James (*whispers to Helen*): I think they want us to leave.
Helen: Well, good-bye.
James: See you later.
Charles and Grace: Good-bye.
(*James and Helen exit right, Charles and Grace exit left.*)

(*At James and Helen's house.*)
(*James and Helen enter right.*)
Helen: They have a lot of nerve. All they wanted was to get
    information from us. They didn't want to play.
James: I guess we're too quaint for them.
Helen: Well, they're too stuck up for me.

James: Rich kids! They've got everything. They don't need us.
(*James and Helen exit right.*)

(*At Charles and Grace's home.*)
(*Charles and Grace enter left.*)
Charles: We've been here one week, and I'm getting bored.
Grace: Me too. We've swum at the best spot, explored among the trees along the shore, and boated with the servants. I'm ready for something else.
Charles: I'd like to meet other kids our age.
Grace: Maybe we should accept Helen's offer and go to church with her and her brother.
Charles: But you already turned down the invitation.
Grace: Maybe they'll ask us again.
Charles: Don't count on it.
Grace: Mother and Father haven't even called yet. I hope they're all right.
Charles: Of course, they are. You know them. They get so wrapped up in their work they forget about us.
Grace: If they'd just call and say hello, it wouldn't take much time, would it?
Charles: They're spending every minute making money for us.
Grace: I don't care about the money. I'd rather have them here.
Charles: Maybe someday we can all vacation together.
Grace: I hope so. (*Charles and Grace exit left.*)

(*At James and Helen's home.*)
(*James and Helen enter right.*)
James: We haven't seen Charles and Grace since the first day they were here.
Helen: They sure are stuck up.
James: Maybe we should ask them over for supper tonight.
Helen: But Uncle John will be here with his slides about missionary work overseas. They won't want to see religious stuff like that.
James: It might be a good way to witness to them.

Helen: They already think we're quaint. They'll think we're real homespun if we tell them about Jesus.

James: Come on, let's ask them anyway.

Helen: You ask them. I'm too scared.

James: Come with me. I'm not doing this alone.

Helen: Are you scared too?

James: I don't like the idea of being called homespun.

Helen: Me neither. So let's forget the whole thing.

James: Maybe you're right. But you know what Uncle John says about witnessing.

Helen: Yeah. He says never let an opportunity to tell about Jesus go by because you may not get another chance.

James: What if they drown while they're swimming? We'd feel awful if we never told them about Jesus.

Helen: They probably know all about Him already.

James: You heard what they said. They haven't been to church since their great-grandma's funeral.

Helen: You've got a point. Maybe God wants us to be the ones to tell them about Jesus.

James: We'd better ask them over right now before we lose our nerve.

Helen: OK. (*James and Helen exit right.*)

(*At Charles and Grace's home.*)

(*James and Helen enter right, Charles and Grace enter left.*)

Grace: Look, it's the quaint little neighbors.

Charles: So it is.

James: Hello.

Helen: Hi.

Charles: What can we do for you?

James: We came over to, uh, invite you to supper tonight.

Helen: Yeah, and you can stay after supper to see Uncle John's slides. He's traveled all over the world.

Charles: How interesting. What line of work is he in?

Helen: He's uh, uh, he's a missionary.

Grace: Goodness! I've never met one of them before.

Charles: It might be interesting.

James: His slides tell about how he shares the gospel of Jesus Christ with people who have never heard it.

Helen: Yeah, his slides are real interesting.

Grace: Well, what do you think, Charles?

Charles: We haven't any other plans. Sure, we'll come.

James: Wonderful!

Helen: That's great!

Grace: This uncle of yours, does he travel all the time?

Helen: Most of the year.

Grace: His family must get lonely.

Helen: Oh, no. They travel with him. In fact, they all help tell about how Jesus died for the sins of the world and that He offers salvation to everyone who will accept Him as their Savior.

Grace: Does he have children?

James: Yes, three of them.

Helen: I do wish our parents would take us on some of their business trips overseas. It gets lonely without them.

James: I have an idea.

Charles: What's that?

James: Let's pray that you and your parents will get to spend more time together.

Grace: Does Jesus answer prayers like that?

Helen: Oh, yes! He cares about every detail of our lives.

James: Would you like to get to know Jesus better?

Charles: Yes.

Grace: So would I.

James: You can, you know. All you have to do is ask Him to come into your heart and forgive your sins. Then you'll be one of His children.

Grace: What do you think, Charles?

Charles: It certainly can't hurt us. Yes, I think we'd like to do that.

James: Wonderful. Let's sit down on the steps over there and pray. (*All exit right.*)

(*At James and Helen's house.*)

(*James and Helen enter right.*)

James: That was so easy.

Helen: And we were too scared to mention Jesus to them at first.

James: We were really dumb, weren't we?

Helen: Yeah. Next time I won't be so scared. Witnessing just takes practice, doesn't it?

James: Right. I feel so happy, my heart may burst. Two more people know Jesus now.

Helen: Wait till we tell Uncle John.

James: Maybe he'll take us on his next missionary trip!

Helen: We don't need to go on a trip. We have a mission field right here at home. (*Both exit center.*)

8
You Lose a Close Relative

Scripture: Matthew 5:4
Props: None
Performance Time: 8 minutes
Characters: David, Curt, Bart, Sally, Mom

(*On the playground.*)
David: Hi, Curt, how'd you do on your social studies test?
Curt: You don't want to know.
David: Yes, I do.
Curt: Well, I don't want to talk about it.
David: That bad, huh?
Curt: Yeah.
David: You've always gotten *A*s and *B*s. What did you do, get a
   C?
Curt: No. I got an, uh, an . . . *F.*
David: You! An *F!* You've never gotten an *F* in your life.
Curt: I know.
David: What happened? Did you forget to study?
Curt: I tried to study, but I couldn't concentrate.
David: Aha! I know the symptoms. You've got a crush on a girl.
   Who is it? Angela?
Curt: I don't have a crush on anybody.
David: You can't fool me.
Curt: Cool it, David, will you?
David: Hey, something's really bothering you, isn't it?
Curt: Yeah, but I don't want to discuss it.

David: I'm your friend. I'd like to help.

Curt: There's nothing you can do.

David: Maybe not, but at least I can listen.

Curt: Did you ever meet my Grandma Taylor?

David: That lady in the wheelchair who's always playing jokes on people?

Curt: Yeah. She died last week.

David: I'm sorry. She was pretty special to you, wasn't she?

Curt: Yes. When Mom and Dad tried to make me throw away my rock collection because they said it made my room too junky, Grandma stood up for me. She knew how important it was to me, and I got to keep it. She even gave me a special rock for Christmas.

David: She sounds like she was a pretty neat lady.

Curt: She was always on my side. All I can do is think about how empty I feel now that she's gone.

David: I have a special grandma too. I'd feel terrible if something happened to her.

Curt: Mom and Dad said she was in lots of pain for several months before she died and now she's free of it. But even when she was hurting, she told jokes and laughed and talked about my rock collection. I think she liked it almost as much as I do.

David: No wonder you got an *F*. No one should have to take a test right after losing someone special.

Curt: The world can't stop because my grandma died. But I don't care about the *F*. I don't care about anything.

David: Your grandma wouldn't want you to think like that. She was proud of how well you did in school. I only met her twice, but both times she told me how smart you were.

Curt: Grandma thought I was pretty special. It made me work harder to please her. Now that she's gone, why should I try anymore?

Bart (*enters right*): Hey, Curt, wait up.

Curt: Oh, no, I don't want to talk to Bart.

David: I thought you were friends. You two run neck and neck in class. You're always vying for the best grades.

Curt: It's a cinch he got a better grade this time, and he'll never let me forget it.

Bart (*approaches Curt and David*): How'd you do on the social studies test, Curt?

Curt: I don't want to talk about it. Let's just say you did better than I did.

Bart: Don't feel bad. It's impossible to beat an *A* plus.

David: Is that what you got?

Bart: Yep.

Curt: You'll probably win the trip to the state capital at the end of the year then.

David: I wish other teachers would be as nice as our social studies teacher. He's given the top student in his class a free trip to the state capital every year since I can remember.

Bart: I've been looking forward to that trip all year, and I'm going to win it.

David: I won't make it. All I get are *B*s and *C*s.

(*Curt starts to move toward the left.*)

Bart: Where are you going?

Curt: Home.

Bart: But you always shoot baskets after school.

Curt: Not today. (*Exits left.*)

Bart: What's wrong with him?

David: His grandmother just died.

Bart (*sarcastically*): And he's brokenhearted.

David: Yeah, you want to make something of it?

Bart: Don't be so touchy.

David: Get lost, you big bag of wind.

Bart: Call me what you want to, but I'm going to the state capital at the end of the year. You wait and see.

David: You're so conceited it's pathetic.

Bart: I heard Curt got an *F* on his test. There's no way he can beat me now. My number one competitor has been sidelined by his dead grandmother. That's a laugh.

David: You're sick, Bart. (*Exits right.*)

Bart: I'm also the top social studies student in the class. So there!
(*Exits center.*)

(*At Curt's house.*)

Sally (*enters right*): Curt, are you coming down for supper?
Mom's called you three times.

Curt (*from offstage*): No. Go away.

Sally: Mom will be mad.

Mom (*enters right*): Come, Sally. Let's eat. Curt needs some time
alone.

Sally: He sure is acting weird.

Mom: He misses Grandma.

Sally: So do I, but I'm not acting weird.

Mom: I miss her too, but Curt's having an extra hard time. We'll
just have to be understanding and love him.

Sally: You know what?

Mom: What?

Sally: He got an *F* on his social studies test today. The whole
school is talking about it. Curt never gets anything below an
A minus.

Mom: Curt got an *F*? Sounds like I'd better have a talk with him.
He must be having an even harder time than I thought.

(*Sally exits right. Mom goes toward left and pretends to knock.*)

Mom: Knock, knock. May I come in?

Curt: Please, Mom, go away.

Mom: I'd really like to talk to you for just a minute. Won't you
let me come in?

Curt: Well, OK, for just a minute. (*Curt enters left.*)

Mom: I heard about your social studies test grade.

Curt: Are you going to ground me?

Mom: No, I don't think that would do any good. You've got a
problem that can't be solved by studying harder.

Curt: I don't care what you do to me. Just do it and get it over
with.

Mom: There's only one thing I can do to help you, Curt, and

that's to love you. You're feeling a lot of pain now. You can't think of anything but losing Grandma. Grades, school, your favorite foods, none of that matters any more.

Curt: That's just how I feel. How did you know?

Mom: Because when I was your age, I lost my grandfather, and he was very special to me too. He always stood up for me when no one else would. If anything upsetting happened, I could go to him and he'd understand. He wouldn't lecture me. He'd just spend time with me, and I knew he loved me as much as I loved him.

Curt: Oh, Mom, it hurts so bad. It's like somebody cut a big piece out of me, and I'll never be whole again.

Mom: That's how I felt. But I can tell you this, Curt. It gets better. You never forget the loss, but it will get easier to remember Grandma without so much pain. One of these days, you'll be able to laugh about the funny things you did together.

Curt: Like the time she and I climbed to the roof with Dad's pajamas and flew them from the TV antenna for April Fool's Day.

Mom: And the time you two put ceramic frogs in the bottom of everyone's tea cups at the church social, and Mrs. Murphy screamed.

Curt: That was so funny I couldn't stop laughing.

Mom: Mrs. Murphy was mad at Grandma for months, but Grandma didn't let that bother her.

Curt: She was so much fun. What will I do without her?

Mom: I can tell you what she'd want you to do.

Curt: What?

Mom: She'd want you to carry on the fun-loving tradition you two shared, and she'd want you to get on with your life. She'd probably say, "Curt, Sonny, you can solve a heap of troubles with a good belly laugh."

Curt: But, Mom, I just can't laugh, not yet.

Mom: You're grieving now, and that's perfectly normal. It's natural to feel nothing matters anymore. But that feeling doesn't last forever. You have to pick up the pieces and get on with your life.

Curt: Grandma would have been pretty upset if she knew I got an *F* on my social studies test.

Mom: You're right. She'd have told you to get up and try again.

Curt: Yeah, she would have! And you know what? I'm going to. I can't let that loud-mouth Bart get the trip to the state capital. I'm going to win that trip for Grandma and me.

Mom: Good for you!

Curt: I'll ask the teacher to let me take the test again or do some makeup work to get rid of that *F*.

Mom: There you go. Grandma would be proud of you.

Curt: Mom, when will it stop hurting so much?

Mom: It took a year before I got over my granddad's death, but each day it got a little better. When the hard times come, think of how many great times you two had together. And then remind yourself that your mom and dad and your sister, Sally, love you a whole lot.

Curt: You won't make me throw away my rock collection now that Grandma's gone, will you?

Mom: No. She made me realize how important it is to you. She taught me a lot too.

Curt: Mom?

Mom: Yes?

Curt: What's for supper?

Mom: That's my boy! I know you're going to make it now.

9
Your Sister Tells
an Embarrassing Secret
About You

Scripture: Proverbs 10:12
Props: None
Performance Time: 7 minutes
Characters: Brian, Martin, Penny, Mom

(*In front of the school.*)
(*Brian and Martin enter left.*)
Brian: I'm never, never going back to school.
Martin: Why?
Brian: My sister, Penny, told a secret about me, and now the whole school is laughing at me.
Martin: I'm not.
Brian: That's because you don't know the secret.
Martin: Yes, I do.
Brian: Oh, no, did Penny tell you too?
Martin: No. I heard it from Dwight and Mary.
Brian: They're not even in our grade! If they know, everyone knows. That does it! I really am never going back to school.
Martin: You have to. If you don't go, you could get in big trouble, and so could your parents.
Brian: Then I'll run away. I hate Penny. Mom and Dad told her never to tell my secret, but she did anyway.
Martin: It's not such a terrible secret.
Brian: Then how come Craig made up that awful rhyme about me? Everyone's saying it.
Martin: I haven't heard it.

Brian: You will. It goes, "Brian, Brian, he's a creep, Sucks his thumb to go to sleep."

Martin: That's kind of cute.

Brian: You call that cute? Get out of here!

Martin: What I mean is, it rhymes and the words sound good together.

Brian: Even my best friend thinks I'm good for a laugh.

Martin: You're taking this too seriously.

Brian: Easy for you to say. How would you feel if your sister told a secret about you that you didn't want anyone to know?

Martin: Pretty mad, I guess.

Brian: Penny better stay out of my way until I cool off, or I might punch her right in the nose.

Martin: I've never seen you so mad.

Brian: That's because I've never had the whole school laughing at me before. The more I think about it, the madder I get. I'm going to find Penny and fix her good. (*Exits right.*)

Martin: Uh, oh! I don't want to be part of that fight. (*Exits left.*)

(*At Brian's house.*)

(*Penny enters left.*)

Brian (*from offstage*): Penny, are you in your room?

Penny: Yeah. Come on in.

Brian: (*enters right*): How could you have done it?

Penny: Done what?

Brian: You know what! You told someone that I suck my thumb at night.

Penny: Oh, that.

Brian: *That* just happens to be a secret Mom and Dad told you not to tell.

Penny: If you weren't such a mean brother, I wouldn't have told.

Brian: What do you mean by that?

Penny: You're the one who called me a chickenbrain at breakfast this morning and an airhead at supper last night and a dumb elephant in front of my best friend, Carol, on the playground day before yesterday.

Brian: That's because you called me names and made me mad.

Penny: I didn't call you names.

Brian: What do you think "stupid ox" is? A friendly greeting?

Penny: That was just a joke. I said it to make people laugh.

Brian: Yeah, laugh at me!

Penny: It worked too.

Brian: I'm going to fix you good. I'll tell everyone you still sleep with your teddy bear.

Penny: You tell that, and you'll be lying. My bear fell apart last year, and Mom threw it away.

Brian: Oh! Then I'll tell them you . . . you, uh, eat spaghetti with your fingers.

Penny: Really, Brian, you're reaching for straws.

Brian: That's it! I'll tell them the only way you'll drink milk is through a straw.

Penny: They'll laugh you out of school if you say that. Lots of other kids do the same thing.

Brian: You just watch out. I'm going to get even with you, and when I do you'll be sorry. I may even sabotage that slumber party you're planning this weekend.

Penny: You wouldn't dare! I've been planning it for weeks. Mom and Dad would really punish you if you mess it up.

Brian: It would be worth it to get my revenge. (*Exits right.*)

Penny: He wouldn't dare. (*Exits left.*)

(*At Brian's house.*)

(*Mom and Brian enter left.*)

Mom: Hurry up, Brian. Finish your cereal or you'll miss the school bus.

Brian: I'm not going to school.

Mom: You most certainly are.

Brian: No, I'm not!

Mom: How come? Are you sick?

Brian: No.

Mom: Then what's wrong?

Brian: All the kids at school are making fun of me. One boy even
    made up a rhyme about me, and everyone's saying it.

Mom: Why are they making fun of you?

Brian: Because Penny told them I suck my thumb to go to sleep
    at night.

Mom: I told her not to tell anyone about that. It's a secret.

Brian: She told anyway. And she's not even sorry.

Mom: I'll have a talk with Penny. In the meantime, you go to
    school. Understand?

Brian: But, Mom!

Mom: No buts, young man! You get on that bus and go to school.
    I'll call the principal later to make sure you got there, so don't
    hide out somewhere.

Brian: Mom! I wouldn't do that.

Mom: Don't "Mom" me. Mind me!

Brian: When will you talk to Penny?

Mom: Today. Now hurry up, or you'll be late.

(*Brian exits right, Mom exits left.*)

(*Later at Brian's house.*)

(*Penny and Mom enter left.*)

Penny: No fair, Mom, you said I could have the slumber party.

Mom: You promised not to tell anyone that Brian sucks his
    thumb at night. Then you broke that promise.

Penny: I only told Sue. She blabbed it all over school.

Mom: Sue would never have blabbed it if you hadn't told her.

Penny: If I apologize, will you let me have my slumber party?
    Please?

Mom: No. Maybe this will teach you that telling secrets is a
    serious thing. You hurt Brian a great deal by revealing his
    secret.

Penny: He called me names first.

Mom: You call him names too. That's no reason to tell secrets
    about him. You know that two wrongs don't make a right.

Penny: I know, I know. But Mom, you don't understand how
    important this slumber party is for me. I went to Carol's and

Sue's slumber parties. If I don't have one for them, they'll never invite me to a slumber party again.

Mom: If they're really your friends, they will. Now go to your room and do your homework.

Penny: You're not being fair.

Mom: Go to your room before I become really mad.

(*Penny exits right, Mom exits left.*)

(*At Brian's house.*)

(*Brian and Mom enter left.*)

Mom: How was school?

Brian: Not so bad. Martin's still my friend, and several kids told me they still suck their thumbs too. I made friends with two of them.

Mom: I'm really glad to hear that.

Brian: Did you talk to Penny?

Mom: Yes.

Brian: What happened?

Mom: That's none of your business. Penny's punishment is between her and me.

Brian: I hope you weren't too hard on her. I'm not mad at her anymore.

Mom: How mad you feel doesn't change the seriousness of what she did. Now run along and do your homework.

(*Mom exits left. Brian walks toward right. He pauses when he hears someone crying.*)

Brian: Is that you, Penny?

Penny (*tearfully from offstage*): Go away! I never want to speak to you again.

Brian: What's wrong?

Penny (*enters right*): It's all your fault.

Brian: What's my fault?

Penny: Mom canceled my slumber party because you said I told about your thumb sucking. Now my friends will never invite me to another slumber party, and they won't like me anymore.

Brian: Then you know how I felt when you told my secret.

Penny: Just go away. (*Exits right.*)

(*Brian walks toward left.*)

Brian: Mom.

Mom (*enters left*): Yes, Brian?

Brian: Did you cancel Penny's slumber party?

Mom: Yes. She has to be punished for telling a secret.

Brian: She thinks she's going to lose all her friends. Please don't punish her so hard.

Mom: You want her to have her party after she told your secret?

Brian: Yes. I've forgiven her.

Mom: That's quite a change of heart from the vengeful boy you were yesterday. How about if we let her have a slumber party later on? She needs to realize she's done a very disloyal thing, so I've got to punish her at least a little.

Brian: Are secrets that important to keep?

Mom: Of course they are! We've got to stick together and love each other, not try to destroy each other.

Brian: Yesterday I felt pretty destroyed, but Martin told me I was taking the whole thing too seriously. I think he was right.

Mom: I'm real glad you're concerned about your sister. It tells me you really care about her.

Brian: I do, Mom, but I sure was mad at her for a while.

Mom: And I was pretty upset with you for acting the way you did. But it looks like we've successfully made it through another family crisis, doesn't it?

Brian: Yeah.

Mom: Let's tell Penny she can have a slumber party next month —and that we love her.

Brian: OK! But let's tell her she has to obey one rule at the party.

Mom: What's that?

Brian: No one can tell secrets about anyone else.

Mom: Right! That's a good rule for all of us all the time.

10
Your Parents Seem to Argue
All the Time

Scripture: Proverbs 3:5-6
Props: Homework paper, a note (Both can be imaginary.)
Performance Time: 12 minutes
Characters: Donna, Mark, Mom, Martha, Mrs. Henderson

(*At Donna and Mark's house.*)
(*Donna and Mark enter center.*)

Donna: Mom and Dad are arguing again, so be real quiet. I don't want them to get madder.

Mark: If you had cleaned up your room when Mom told you to, maybe she wouldn't be upset.

Donna: Don't blame me! You're the one who spilled milk all over the dining room table this morning, and Dad had to change his clothes before he went to work.

Mark: If you think they're arguing because I spilled the milk, you're crazy.

Donna: Then why do you think they're arguing?

Mark: Probably because you're such a creep.

Donna: Maybe it is my fault.

Mark: Come on, I was only kidding. I don't know why they argue all the time.

Donna: It scares me.

Mark: Me too.

Donna: I don't want to think about it anymore. I'm going to put cotton balls in my ears and try to do my homework.

Mark: I got an *F* on my last homework assignment in math.

Donna: Uh oh!

Mark: I did the homework, but I couldn't concentrate on the story problems. Mom and Dad were arguing so loudly I could hear every word they said, even though they were downstairs in the living room and I was upstairs in my bedroom.

Donna: Come on, I'll get you some cotton balls so you can do your homework. (*Both exit center.*)

(*In Mark's classroom.*)

(*Mrs. Henderson and Mark enter center.*)

Mrs. Henderson: Mark, I want you to stay after school.

Mark: Yes, Ma'am.

Mrs. Henderson: Go tell your sister you'll be late, then come back to class.

Mark: OK. (*Mark exits left.*)

Mrs. Henderson: I don't know what I'm going to do with that boy. He used to get *A*s and *B*s in math. Now all he gets are *D*s and *F*s.

Mark (*reenters left*): I'm back.

Mrs. Henderson: Let's talk about your homework assignment.

Mark: I tried real hard, Mrs. Henderson.

Mrs. Henderson: I've just finished grading it. Here, you take a look at it.

Mark: Uh oh! You have every problem marked wrong.

Mrs. Henderson: That's right. You got an *F*.

Mark: Sorry. I really tried.

Mrs. Henderson: Something's wrong, isn't it? If you want to talk about it, I want to listen.

Mark: Uh, nothing's wrong, really. I guess math is just getting too hard for me.

Mrs. Henderson: Math is your best subject. You've already mastered the concepts in these story problems, and you have lots of *A*s and *B*s to prove it. But suddenly, you're failing all the time. I've been a teacher many years, Mark, and I know when something's bothering my students.

Mark: I guess I'm just worried because of all the *F*s I've been getting.

Mrs. Henderson: I'm worried too. We're far enough along in the year that your past good grades will keep you from failing math. But what really concerns me is that you're carrying around a load of worry that's too heavy for you. I'd like to help lighten that load if I can.

Mark: Thanks, Mrs. Henderson. You're really a nice teacher, but there's nothing you can do.

Mrs. Henderson: Well, if you decide to talk about it, I'll be here.

Mark: Thanks. May I go now?

Mrs. Henderson: Not yet. I want you to do the homework assignment for tonight at your desk right now. Maybe if you do it here, you'll be able to concentrate better.

Mark: OK.

(*Mark works quietly and quickly for a few seconds.*)

Mark: I'm all finished.

Mrs. Henderson: Good. Now let me grade your paper before you leave. (*She pretends to grade the paper.*) My, my, this is wonderful. You made an *A!*

Mark: I did?

Mrs. Henderson: Yes. You got every problem right. That makes me think whatever is bothering you must be happening at home, maybe while you're trying to do your homework. Am I right?

Mark: Well, uh . . .

Mrs. Henderson: You don't have to talk about it if you don't want to. But I care, and I'd like to help.

Mark: Thanks. May I go now?

Mrs. Henderson: Yes.

(*Mark exits left, Mrs. Henderson exits center.*)

(*At Mark and Donna's house.*)

(*Mom enters center, Mark enters left.*)

Mom: You're late, Mark. What kept you so long at school?

Mark: Mrs. Henderson made me do my homework at school.

Mom: Why?

Mark: Because I get *F*s when I do it at home.

Mom: Oh, dear. Well, how did you do?

Mark: I got an *A*!

Mom: Good for you!

Mark: Where's Dad?

Mom: He had to work late. So it will be just you, Donna, and me for supper.

Mark: Good!

Mom: Don't you like to eat supper with your dad?

Mark: Uh, sure, it's just that, well, if he's not here, uh, you two won't get into an argument.

Mom: Oh, come on, we don't argue that much.

Mark: Only every day.

Mom: Well, don't let it bother you. We may disagree, but we love each other very much.

Mark: Are you and Dad going to get a divorce?

Mom: Where did you get a silly idea like that?

Mark: You never have fun together anymore. All you do is argue.

Mom: We're a family, Honey, and families stick together. Quit worrying about your dad and me.

(*Mark exits left, Donna enters right.*)

Donna: Was that Mark?

Mom: Yes, he finally got home from school.

Donna: What took him so long?

Mom: His teacher made him do his homework at school because he's been getting bad grades.

Donna: I've been trying really hard to get good grades.

Mom: I've noticed. You're having a very good year.

Donna: Can I help you fix supper? I've already finished vacuuming all the carpets.

Mom: Thanks, Donna, but supper's all ready. Wash your hands, call Mark, and we'll eat.

Donna: What about Dad?

Mom: He's working late.

Donna: Again? He sure has been working late a lot lately. Doesn't he like to have us around anymore?

Mom: Of course, he does. His job is just very demanding right now.

Donna: It's never been this demanding before.

Mom: He has more responsibilities since he got that promotion. Stop worrying about Dad. He loves you. That's why he's working so hard.

Donna: Sure, Mom. I'll get Mark.

(*Donna exits right, Mom exits center.*)

(*On playground.*)

(*Martha and Donna enter center.*)

Martha: Donna, want to come over to my house after school and play?

Donna: I'd like to, Martha, but I have to go right home.

Martha: Can't you play for just a little while?

Donna: No, I really have to get home.

Martha: What's gotten into you lately? All you ever do is go home right after school. You don't go anywhere or do anything like you used to.

Donna: It's taking more time to keep up with my homework. I've gotten all *A*s so far this year. I don't want to blow it.

Martha: Well, you sure are acting different. Is anything wrong?

Donna: I'm all right.

Martha: Are you sure?

Donna: Well, uh, it's hard to talk about.

Martha: I'm your best friend, and I don't tell secrets. You can trust me.

Donna: I know.

Martha: So what's wrong?

Donna: It's . . . it's my parents. They fight all the time, and Dad stays late at work most of the week. It's like he doesn't love us anymore.

Martha: Is that what's bothering you?

Donna: Yeah. I figure if I get straight *A*s in school, it will help my parents be happy and quit arguing. Then maybe they'll love me again.

Martha: You poor thing. You know who you sound like?

Donna: Who?

Martha: Me, last year. My parents were having problems then.

Donna: What happened?

Martha: They went to a marriage counselor our pastor recommended, and they're doing fine now.

Donna: My dad's so busy he wouldn't have time to see a counselor. I'll just keep on working extra hard in school and at home to make it easier for him.

Martha: You can study as hard as you want and help out at home until your knuckles get raw, but it won't change the way your parents are acting. They're not arguing because of you.

Donna: How do you know?

Martha: That's how parents are. I know. I've been through this. Your parents are having trouble with each other, not with you. Why don't you give them the name of my parents' counselor? Maybe they'll surprise you and go to see her.

Donna: OK, I guess.

Martha: Here it is.

Donna: Thanks. See you tomorrow.

(*Donna and Martha exit center.*)

(*At Donna and Mark's home.*)

(*Donna and Mark enter center.*)

Donna: Hi, Mark. Where are Mom and Dad?

Mark: In the kitchen. They're arguing again.

Donna: Oh, dear.

Mark: I don't know what to do. I got an *A* on my homework. I cleaned up my room. I even set the table for supper, and they're still arguing.

Donna: I know what you mean. I've gotten all *A*s in school this year, and I help Mom and Dad a lot with the housework and yardwork. But it doesn't seem to do any good.

Mark: Maybe if we stayed with Grandma a while, they'd get along better without us.

Donna: Grandma's been sick. She couldn't take care of us.

Mark: Maybe we could live with Uncle Henry and Aunt Wilma for a while.

Donna: They're getting ready to move. They'll be so busy packing and unpacking they won't have time for us.

Mark: How about Uncle Jack and Aunt Minnie?

Donna: They wouldn't know what to do with us because they don't have any kids. Besides, I don't think they like children very well.

Mark: Then maybe we should just run away.

Donna: There's got to be a better solution than that.

Mark: My teacher said she'd help me if she could. Maybe we should talk to her.

Donna: Did you tell her about Mom and Dad?

Mark: No.

Donna: Good. It's none of her business.

Mark: But if we don't talk to her, where will we get help for Mom and Dad?

Donna: I don't know. Maybe there's nothing we can do.

Mark: Mrs. Henderson's really nice. Why don't you come to my classroom after school? You can talk to her about anything. If you think you can trust her, we can tell her about Mom and Dad.

Donna: Well, OK.

(*Donna and Mark exit center.*)

(*In Mark's classroom.*)

(*Mrs. Henderson enters left, Donna and Mark enter center.*)

Mark: Mrs. Henderson, this is my big sister, Donna.

Mrs. Henderson: Hi, Donna. How are you?

Donna: Fine.

Mrs. Henderson: I'll be here a while after school, so you're welcome to stay as long as I'm here.

Donna: Thanks. I just thought I'd drop by and meet Mark's teacher.

Mrs. Henderson: Mark is one of my best math students.

Mark: Thanks.

Donna: Do you know how to crochet?

Mrs. Henderson: No, but I admire people who can.

Donna: Oh, well, do you like to, uh, uh, bake cookies?

Mrs. Henderson: I sure do. Chocolate-chip cookies are my favorites. But everyone else in the family likes them too. I'm lucky if I get to eat even one before they're all gone.

Donna: Do you have any children?

Mrs. Henderson: I have three. John is a senior in high school. Steve is a sophomore, and Debbie is in seventh grade.

Donna: Oh? Do they have a daddy?

Mrs. Henderson: Yes. His name is Peter, and we all live together in a house just a few blocks from here.

Donna: Uh, does Mr. Henderson sometimes come home late from work?

Mrs. Henderson: Every once in a while, but not very often.

Donna: Well, uh, do you two argue a lot?

Mrs. Henderson: Sometimes we disagree, but we don't argue much at our house. We usually settle our problems by talking them out together.

Donna: Oh!

Mrs. Henderson: Is something special on your mind, Donna, that you'd like to talk about?

Donna: Uh, no, no, of course not.

Mrs. Henderson: I know Mark has been having problems at home. He hasn't told me what they are, but I think I can guess. If you need someone to talk to, I'm here.

Mark: Go ahead, Donna, tell her.

Donna: Well, uh, Mrs. Henderson, see, it's just that, well, we don't think our parents love us anymore.

Mrs. Henderson: Why do you say that?

Donna: They argue with each other all the time, and Dad gets home late from work almost every day. No matter how hard we try to do well in school and help out at home, it doesn't do any good.

Mark: Do you think we should run away?

Mrs. Henderson: No, that would only make things worse. I don't know your parents, but I'm sure they love you. They're having problems getting along with each other, not with you.

Donna: But maybe we're making the problem worse. If we went away for a while . . .

Mrs. Henderson: Believe, me, that wouldn't help.

Donna: How do you know?

Mrs. Henderson: I've been a teacher many years, and I've seen these same symptoms time and again in children who attend my class. It's usually the same problem. Their parents argue a lot and don't get along, and the children think it's their fault. They think if they act like perfect angels or leave home for a while, their parents will get along better and everything will be all right again. But it never works that way.

Donna: It doesn't?

Mrs. Henderson: No, because the children usually aren't the cause of their parents' problems.

Donna: What happened to the kids in your class who had a problem like ours?

Mrs. Henderson: When they realized the problems their parents had weren't the students' fault, the kids began to improve.

Donna: Are you saying we can't do anything to change the way our parents are behaving?

Mrs. Henderson: That's right.

Mark: That makes me feel so helpless.

Mrs. Henderson: Well, there is one thing you can do.

Mark: What?

Mrs. Henderson: You can pray.

Donna: We've been doing that.

Mrs. Henderson: You can do something else too. You can let me talk with your parents, tell them how their problems are affecting you, and suggest they get help.

Donna: That might make them mad at us.

Mark: They might even argue more.

Mrs. Henderson: They need help. Do you think they'll get it by themselves?

Donna: Probably not.

Mark: I don't want them to get a divorce. My friend Billy's parents got a divorce, and he hates it.

Donna: I guess you can talk to Mom and Dad. Maybe only Mom because Dad is so busy at work. Here, I've got the name of a good counselor who helped my friend Martha's parents when they had problems.

Mrs. Henderson: I know this counselor. She's very good. Don't you worry. I'll arrange everything. If you need to talk some more, you know where to come.

Mark: Thanks.

Donna: We'd better go now.

(*Donna and Mark exit center, Mrs. Henderson exits left.*)

(*On the playground.*)

(*Martha and Donna enter center.*)

Martha: Hi, Donna.

Donna: Hi.

Martha: You look happy.

Donna: I feel great.

Martha: How's everything at home?

Donna: Better. My parents aren't arguing as much, and Dad's coming home from work in time to eat supper with us.

Martha: What happened to make them change?

Donna: They're going to that marriage counselor your parents went to. Mark and I talk to her sometimes too. Mom and Dad still have some problems, but I think they're going to work them out. And I found out they still love me.

Martha: Of course, they do. I told you that.

Donna: Mark and I thought they were arguing because we were doing something wrong. But we found out that wasn't true.

Martha: I'm glad you're all doing better.

Donna: Mom and Dad still argue sometimes, and I suppose

they'll see the counselor for several more months. But whatever happens, it sure feels good to know their problems aren't my fault.

Martha: Want to come over to my house and play games for a while?

Donna: Sure. Mark can walk home from school by himself. He's doing better now. He even gets As and Bs on the homework he does at home. And I can relax and spend some time playing with my friends because it's up to my parents—not me, to work out their problems.

Martha: Hooray for you! Let's go.

(*Martha and Donna exit center.*)

11
You Move to a New Neighborhood

Scripture: Isaiah 55:12
Props: One bat, one softball, eight snowballs (All can be imaginary.)
Performance Time: 8 minutes
Characters: Henry, Jerry, Sheila, George, Andy, Morgan

(*At Henry's house.*)
(*Henry and Jerry enter center.*)
Henry: Do you want my big stuffed bear?
Jerry: Sure!
Henry: How about my erector set?
Jerry: Wow! You mean it?
Henry: Yeah. They're yours.
Jerry: How come you're giving away such neat toys?
Henry: I have to. We're moving.
Jerry: You mean I won't get to play with you anymore?
Henry: That's right. I don't want to move, but Dad got this good job in another state.
Jerry: I wish you didn't have to go. You're my best friend.
Henry: We've been best friends since we were two years old and you moved next door to me. I'll never find a better friend.
Jerry: I'm really going to miss you. When do you have to leave?
Henry: Tomorrow.
Jerry: That hardly gives us time to say good-bye.
Henry: I know. It's awful, isn't it?

Jerry: I've got an idea. Come over to my house. I'll hide you so no one can find you. Your folks won't leave without you.

Henry: That might work for a day or two, but our parents would find us sooner or later.

Jerry: I guess so. Well, you'll have to call sometimes and tell me how things are going.

Henry: And you'll have to tell me who takes my place as pitcher on the school softball team. I really thought we could be the top team in the league this year.

Jerry: Me too. You're the best pitcher we have. Without you, I'm not sure we'll do well.

Henry: I wish I didn't have to go. It's going to be hard starting over somewhere new.

Jerry: You'll do all right.

(*Jerry and Henry exit center.*)

(*At Henry's new home.*)

(*Henry and Sheila enter center.*)

Henry: This house is gigantic.

Sheila: I like it! I have a huge bedroom all to myself.

Henry: My bedroom's pretty big too, and it has a window facing the street. Now I can see what's going on outside all the time.

Sheila: Do you like it better than our old house?

Henry: No. There, I knew all the good hideouts and all the floor boards that squeaked. And my best friend, Jerry, lived next door.

Sheila: Are you ready for school tomorrow?

Henry: No. I've never gone to a school where I didn't know anyone.

Sheila: Me either. I'm sort of scared, but maybe we'll meet some nice kids.

Henry: I hope so.

(*Henry and Sheila exit center.*)

(*At school*)

(*George and Andy enter left, Henry enters center.*)

George: What have we here?

Andy: Looks like a new kid to me.

George: We'll have to break him in real quick, won't we?

Andy: Yeah. Let's give him his first lesson right now. Hey, kid.
    See that piece of paper? Pick it up.

Henry: Pick it up yourself.

Andy: A smart mouth, huh?

George: We'll have to take him down a notch or two.

Andy: I said pick it up.

Henry: Bug off, will you?

George: He needs a knuckle sandwich in the chops.

Andy: Right. Show him your fist.

(*Morgan enters right.*)

Morgan: Who are you two picking on now?

Andy: What's it to you?

Morgan: Nothing. I just wondered.

George: There's a new kid in school. We're showing him who's
    boss.

Morgan: Hi. What's your name?

Henry: Henry.

Morgan: I'm Morgan. You good at anything?

Henry: I play softball some.

Morgan: All right! We need a good batter. He sounds OK to me,
    guys. Come on, Henry, I'll show you around.

George: Party pooper.

Andy: We were just getting ready to have some fun with him.

Morgan: He's with me. You mess with him, and you've got me
    to answer to. Get it?

George and Andy: Yeah, yeah.

(*George and Andy exit left.*)

Henry: Thanks.

Morgan: It was nothing. You've just got to know how to talk to
    those two.

Henry: Is this a pretty tough neighborhood?

Morgan: Only to newcomers. Once you're in, everything's cool.

Henry: This is my first day at school here. You're the only friendly person I've met.

Morgan: You play softball, huh?

Henry: Yeah.

Morgan: We have a team that plays after school. Show us what you can do at bat. If you're good, you'll have no problem fitting in. We're big softball fans.

Henry: I'm not so good at bat. I'm better at pi . . .

Morgan: I'll decide if you're a good batter or not.

(*Morgan exits right.*)

Henry (*calls after him*): I'm better at pitching. (*Shrugs.*) I guess he didn't hear me.

(*Henry exits center.*)

(*On the softball field after school.*)

(*Morgan and Henry enter center.*)

Morgan: Hey, kid, I thought you said you were good at softball.

Henry: I told you I wasn't real good at batting. Give me another chance.

Morgan: OK, but you mess this one up, and you're off the team.

Henry: I'm ready.

Morgan: You'd better be. The pitcher's winding up his arm.

(*Henry pretends to swing at a ball.*)

Morgan: You missed! You're off the team.

Henry: One more chance, please?

Morgan: Forget it. You don't cut the mustard. Now get lost!

(*Henry looks defeated. Morgan exits center, Henry exits left.*)

(*At Henry and Sheila's new home.*)

(*Henry and Sheila enter center.*)

Sheila: How'd it go today?

Henry: Terrible. I thought I'd found a friend, but he turned out to be a jerk, just like all the other kids.

Sheila: I'm sorry.

Henry: You sound happy. Things must have gone well for you.

Sheila: I hate to bring it up when you're so sad, but, yes, they did.

I found two new friends. We sit together in class, and they don't live very far from our new home.

Henry: At least one of us had a good day. I think I'll ask Mom and Dad if I can go back and live with Jerry and his family. Think they'll let me?

Sheila: Not a chance.

Henry: I hate school. I hate this new neighborhood. Why did Mom and Dad have to move, anyway?

Sheila: Dad really likes his new job, and he's getting a lot more money. And Mom has a part-time job at the library. She really loves it.

Henry: Looks like everybody's settled in but me.

Sheila: Give yourself time. It will get better.

Henry: Sure! Tell me another one.

(*Sheila and Henry exit center.*)

(*Near the school next morning. A light snow is on the ground.*)

(*George and Andy enter right. Henry enters left.*)

George: Hey, Andy, there's that new kid walking to school.

Andy: Let's throw snowballs at him.

George: Good idea. (*George and Andy each throw a snowball.*)

Henry: Hey, who threw those snowballs?

George: Smack, right in the face! Good aim, Andy.

Henry: I'm warning you. Don't do it again.

Andy: Ready, aim, fire! (*Throws another snowball.*)

Henry: That does it. I warned you. (*Throws several snowballs, hitting George and Andy each time.*)

George: Hey, let's get out of here. That kid's good. He's thrown five snowballs and hit us every time.

Andy: He's no fun to tease, anyway.

(*George and Andy exit right.*)

Henry: What a bunch of jerks. I hate this place.

(*Henry exits left.*)

(*On the playground later that day.*)

(*Morgan, George, and Andy enter right. Henry enters left.*)

Morgan: Hey, Henry, come over here. We need another person for our four-square game.

Henry: I don't feel like playing.

Morgan: Come on. It beats sitting by the fence doing nothing.

Henry: Leave me alone.

Morgan: Suit yourself. Guess we'll have to find something else to play. Anyone for softball?

George: Sure.

Andy: Yeah, I'll play.

Morgan: I'll pitch. You bat, George, and you catch, Andy.

Andy: Here's the ball. (*Throws it to Morgan. Morgan pitches it to George.*)

George: That was a lousy pitch. Can't you do any better?

Morgan: Quit complaining. I'm just getting warmed up. (*He throws the ball again.*)

George: That pitch was worse than the first. I don't want to play anymore. It's no fun without a good pitcher.

Morgan: Hey, I'm doing my best.

George: It's not good enough. I'm quitting.

Andy: Wait a minute! Remember the snowballs this morning?

George: Yeah. That new kid sure clobbered us. Maybe he'd be a good pitcher.

Morgan: He was lousy at bat yesterday.

Andy: Give him a chance. He can't be any worse than you are.

Morgan: OK, OK. Henry, want to pitch?

Henry: Leave me alone.

Morgan: We need you. George and Andy say you're pretty good at throwing. Show us what you can do.

Henry: George and Andy said that?

Morgan: Yes. Come on, show us your arm.

(*Morgan throws Henry the ball.*)

Henry: Well, uh, OK.

George: Give me all you've got.

Henry: Here comes. (*Pitches the ball.*)

Andy: Wow! Did you see that?

Morgan: Strike one!

Henry: Ready?

George: Yeah.

(*Henry pitches again.*)

Morgan: Strike two!

Henry: Here comes the ball.

George: I'm ready this time.

(*Henry pitches.*)

Andy: Wow!

Morgan: Strike three, you're out!

George: Good grief, he's good.

Morgan: Why didn't you tell me you were a pitcher yesterday?

Henry: I tried, but you wouldn't listen.

Morgan: You're better than our best pitcher. We might win big in the softball league this year if you pitch for our team.

George: Yeah. You've got a place on the team if you want it.

Morgan: What do you say?

Henry: I say you've got a lousy way of welcoming new kids to school. But I like to pitch, so I'll join the team.

Morgan: I guess we were kind of hard on you.

George: Sorry, Henry, but this is a tough place. It's just the way we've learned to act.

Andy: You're one of us now. We'll treat you better.

Henry: Just go a little easier on the next new kid who comes along, OK?

Morgan: We're really pretty nice once you get to know us.

Henry: When's your next softball practice?

Morgan: After school tomorrow.

Henry: I'll see you there.

George, Andy, and Morgan: OK.

(*All exit center.*)

(*At Henry and Sheila's house.*)

Sheila: You look like a different person today.

Henry: I've made some friends, even though they were pretty mean at first.

Sheila: Think you'll stick around for a while?

Henry: Yeah. Jerry doesn't need me living with him and his family. But the softball team at school needs a pitcher, and they've chosen me.

Sheila: Wonderful! You do have a pretty good arm.

Henry: I'm going to use it for more than pitching. The next new boy that comes to school, I'm going to shake his hand and let him know he has a friend.

Sheila: You're all right for a kid brother.

(Henry and Sheila exit center.)

12
You Know You Should Tithe, but Don't Think You Can Afford To

Scripture: Malachi 3:10
Props: Two hair bows, offering envelope
Performance Time: 8 minutes
Characters: Carol, Jill

(*Outside church.*)
(*Carol and Jill enter center.*)
Carol: Hi, Jill. Ready for Sunday School?
Jill: I guess so.
Carol: You sound like you don't want to go.
Jill: I don't.
Carol: Why?
Jill: Because it's too embarrassing.
Carol: What's embarrassing about Sunday School, for heaven's sake?
Jill: You wouldn't understand. Your parents have lots of money.
Carol: What do my parents have to do with this? They aren't in our class.
Jill: But they give you money to put in the offering plate.
Carol: They do not.
Jill: They do too.
Carol: No, they don't.
Jill: Then where do you get the money you put in the offering every Sunday?
Carol: I save it from my allowance.
Jill: Then your parents do give it to you.

Carol: Sure, they give me an allowance, but it's just three dollars a week. I save 10 percent of it to put in the offering.

Jill: Three dollars?

Carol: Yeah. And every week I put thirty cents in the offering plate.

Jill: Are you sure that's all you get?

Carol: Yes! Why are you having such a hard time believing me?

Jill: Because I get three dollars a week too. But I can't afford to tithe.

Carol: Is that why you don't want to go to Sunday School? Because you're embarrassed not to have money for the offering?

Jill: Yeah.

Carol: No one's going to condemn you if you don't put money in the offering plate.

Jill: But they'll notice, and that makes me feel funny.

Carol: You know what the Bible says. We're supposed to tithe 10 percent of what we have. But God won't disown you if you don't.

Jill: I know. But I still wish I had enough money to put in my share.

Carol: Maybe you just need a little help.

Jill: I don't think anyone can help. When there's not enough money, you can't create more out of thin air.

Carol: If we figure out how you spend your money, maybe we can find out how to save enough so you can tithe.

Jill: Well, maybe. Let's see. Mom and Dad give me my allowance every Saturday morning. I put it in my purse, and then sometimes we go shopping.

Carol: Did you go shopping last Saturday?

Jill: Yeah.

Carol: Did you spend any money?

Jill: I bought this cute little doll. It cost two dollars and forty cents. Then I bought a cookie for sixty cents, and all my money was gone.

Carol: Oops. What did you do for money the rest of the week?

Jill: I didn't have any to spend. I needed a new pencil for school, but Dad bought me that.

Carol: Did you have fun playing with the doll you bought?

Jill: For a day or two. Then I got bored with it. It didn't seem as neat as it did when I saw it in the store.

Carol: What about the cookie?

Jill: It was good! But Mom made some at home that were even better.

Carol: There may be a simple solution to your problem.

Jill: Don't tell me to stop going to the store.

Carol: I won't. Maybe you should do what I do with my money.

Jill: What's that?

Carol: I put one dollar in my piggy bank so I can save it for something special. Then I put thirty cents in an offering envelope so it's all ready for Sunday School. That leaves me one dollar and seventy cents for whatever I want to do with it.

Jill: Sounds like a lot of work and bother to me.

Carol: It's easy once you get the hang of it. And I have enough money left over to buy a few things during the week. I could use more money, though, so I'm trying to talk Mom and Dad into giving me four dollars a week.

Jill: Good luck!

Carol: With four dollars a week, I'd have enough money to splurge on my favorite food every now and then.

Jill: What's that?

Carol: Chocolate sundaes. Yum!

Jill: My folks would have a good laugh if I asked for more money. They think I'm careless with what I get now.

Carol: That gives me an idea.

Jill: What?

Carol: It's a way to get your allowance increased and give you enough money to tithe in Sunday School.

Jill: Wow! Let's hear the details.

Carol: Tell your folks that you're going to manage your money better because you want to have enough to tithe.

Jill: They wouldn't believe me.

Carol: Tell them anyway. Then prove to them you can do it.

Jill: How?

Carol: By putting a dollar in your piggy bank to save for something special and by putting thirty cents in your tithing envelope as soon as you get your allowance. Then use the money you have left over for things you really need. If you follow my plan, I guarantee your parents will be impressed.

Jill: You think so?

Carol: I know so.

Jill: OK. I'll try it.

Carol: We'll talk next week and see how you did.

(*Carol and Jill exit center.*)

(*Next Sunday outside church.*)

(*Jill and Carol enter center.*)

Carol: Hi, Jill. I like those bows in your hair.

Jill: Thanks.

Carol: Where did you get them?

Jill: I bought them at the store.

Carol: With your allowance money?

Jill: Yeah. They cost one dollar and fifty cents each.

Carol: Uh oh. Then you don't have any money for the Sunday School offering today.

Jill: I couldn't help it. I saw these beautiful bows, and they just begged me to buy them.

Carol: What did your parents say about that?

Jill: Mom said she didn't think I'd ever learn to manage my money no matter how hard I tried, and Dad agreed.

Carol: You'll just have to try again. Remember, this won't be easy. You've got to learn to resist the temptation to buy everything that grabs your fancy.

Jill: You sound just like my parents.

Carol: Don't give up now. You want to have money for the offering, don't you?

Jill: Yes.

Carol: Come on, then. Try for another week. We'll talk next
    Sunday and see how you did.

Jill: OK.

(*Carol and Jill exit center.*)

(*Next week outside church.*)

(*Carol and Jill enter center.*)

Carol: Hi, Jill. How'd you do this week?

Jill: See this?

Carol: Yeah. What is it?

Jill: My offering envelope.

Carol: Good for you!

Jill: Well, sort of good for me. It only has ten cents in it.

Carol: How come only ten cents?

Jill: Well, see, I was in the store and saw this great set of jacks
    with a superneat ball. I just had to have it because I lost two
    jacks and a ball from my old set. So I bought it, but I had
    to use some of my offering money to pay for it.

Carol: If you had saved your money for another week, you
    wouldn't have had to use your tithing money to buy the jacks.
    But you're doing better. At least today you can put a little
    money in the offering plate.

Jill: Yeah. Well, let's talk again next week.

(*Carol and Jill exit center.*)

(*Next week outside church.*)

(*Carol and Jill enter center.*)

Jill: Hi, Carol!

Carol: You sound excited.

Jill: See this?

Carol: Your offering envelope?

Jill: Yep. Know what's in it?

Carol: Thirty cents?

Jill: Nope.

Carol: Twenty cents?

Jill: Nope. Guess again.

Carol: Ten cents.

Jill: Nope.

Carol: I give up. What's in your envelope?

Jill: Fifty cents! Thirty cents for this week and twenty cents for the money I was short last week.

Carol: Wow! How'd you do it?

Jill: I resisted the impulse to buy, like you said, and I saved my money. By the end of the week, I had a whole dollar left. So I put fifty cents in the offering envelope, and I used the other fifty cents to buy some candy.

Carol: Candy?

Jill: You can't expect me to resist everything, can you? That candy was just calling to me. I couldn't turn it down.

Carol: You deserve a reward for doing so well with your money.

Jill: See you next week. Maybe I'll have big news for you then.

Carol: Big news, huh? OK.

(*Jill and Carol exit center.*)

(*Next week outside church.*)

(*Jill and Carol enter center.*)

Carol: Hi, Jill.

Jill: Hi. Have I got news for you!

Carol: What?

Jill: My parents are so impressed with the way I've been saving my money that they raised my allowance to four dollars!

Carol: Four dollars! You lucky duck. I still get only three dollars a week.

Jill: And look here.

Carol: Your offering envelope?

Jill: Yep. Know what's in it?

Carol: Thirty cents?

Jill: Nope. Forty cents because 10 percent of four dollars is forty cents.

Carol: Good for you.

Jill: And you know what's in my pocket?

Carol: What?

Jill: Two dollars.

Carol: Don't let it burn a hole in your pocket.

Jill: Know what I'm going to do with it?

Carol: What?

Jill: I'm going to treat you to a chocolate sundae.

Carol: Wow! But why are you being so generous?

Jill: Because you taught me an important lesson about how to handle my money.

Carol: That's really nice of you. Thanks.

Jill: You're welcome.

Carol: Say, can I ask you a question?

Jill: Sure.

Carol: Think you could lend me a dollar?

Jill: What for?

Carol: Well, I saw this really neat bracelet in the store, and all I need is one more dollar before I can buy it.

Jill: Friend to friend, Carol, let me give you some advice.

Carol: What?

Jill: You've got to resist the temptation to buy everything that grabs your fancy.

Carol: That's the advice I gave you!

Jill: It was pretty good advice too.

Carol: Oh, you! But you're right. If I wait until next week, I'll have the money to buy that bracelet.

Jill: That's the spirit.

Carol: Come on, let's go to Sunday School so we can put our money in the offering plate. And tomorrow you can treat me to that chocolate sundae.

(*Jill and Carol exit center.*)

13
You Take Something that Isn't Yours

Scripture: Ephesians 4:28
Props: Four wood plaques, sack (All can be imaginary.)
Performance Time: 11 minutes
Characters: Jeremy, Michael, Dad, Calvin, Jenny

(*On sidewalk.*)
(*Jeremy enters left, Michael enters right.*)
Jeremy: Where are you going so fast?
Michael: To my grandma's house. I'm supposed to help her make pipe-cleaner animals for the church craft sale. We're raising money for the world hunger cause.
Jeremy: That sounds hard.
Michael: It's not bad. I mostly do the easy stuff. Grandma shapes the legs, head, and tails to make them look like real animals.
Jeremy: Can I come too?
Michael: Grandma's house is pretty small, and we have stuff scattered all over. You'd better wait until I ask Grandma if it's all right.
Jeremy: Oh, never mind. I need to get home anyway.
Michael: What are you going to make for the craft sale?
Jeremy: My mom is baking cookies, and my sister's making fudge. But I'm not making anything. I'm too clumsy.
Michael: You are not. You ought to try to make something. It's really fun.
Jeremy: I guess I could make something really neat if I had someone to help me.

Michael: Well, gotta go. See you later.

Jeremy: Bye.

(*Michael exits center.*)

Jeremy: I wonder if I could talk Dad into helping me make something for the craft sale.

(*Jeremy exits center.*)

(*At Jeremy's house.*)

(*Jeremy enters center, Dad enters left.*)

Dad: Hi, Son. What are you up to?

Jeremy: I was thinking about the church craft sale.

Dad: It's only two days away.

Jeremy: I know. Mom and Jenny are making cookies and fudge for the craft sale. Do you think you and I could make something too?

Dad: That sounds like a great idea, Jeremy, but I can't do it. I'm really swamped at work, and I have to go back tonight for an important meeting.

Jeremy: Well, could you at least give me some ideas for something I could do?

Dad: Let's see. You could make some little matchstick cars.

Jeremy: That would take too long.

Dad: You could make some toothpick figures.

Jeremy: I'm lousy at things like that.

Dad: How about painting some rocks for paperweights?

Jeremy: Well, maybe.

Dad: We have plenty of rocks to choose from in the backyard, and I have some cans of paint in the garage you can use.

Jeremy: I'll think about it.

Dad: Wish I could stay and help, but I have to go.

Jeremy: Bye.

(*Dad exits left.*)

Jeremy: I don't want to make rock paperweights all by myself. Besides, it sounds like too much work. I think I'll go visit Calvin next door.

(*Jeremy walks toward right.*)

Jeremy: Knock, knock.
(*Calvin enters right.*)
Calvin: Oh, it's you.
Jeremy: Can you play with me?
Calvin: Sure. I just finished painting short Scripture verses on the last pieces of wood. Now they're drying, so I can play.
Jeremy: Why are you painting verses on wood?
Calvin: They're presents for my cousins and aunts and uncles for Christmas. I have to start early because I have lots of relatives.
Jeremy: Wow. How many pieces of wood did you paint?
Calvin: Twenty.
Jeremy: That must have taken forever.
Calvin: Over a month. I sure am glad I'm done. Want to come out to the garage and see them?
Jeremy: Sure.
(*Calvin and Jeremy walk toward left.*)
Calvin: There they are.
Jeremy: Ooh! They're really neat. Your relatives will like them.
Calvin: I hope so. Oops, I just forgot. I'm supposed to pick up milk and eggs for Mom at the store. I'd better go. Look at the plaques as long as you want to.
Jeremy: OK. Thanks.
(*Calvin exits right.*)
Jeremy: Twenty plaques! Wow! They sure would make nice craft sale items. I'll bet Calvin wouldn't mind if I took three or four to sell at our church craft sale. He's got so many, he won't miss a few. Besides, we're friends, and he'd want me to have them. Let's see, which ones do I like best? I think I'll take these four right here. People will really be impressed when they see what I'm taking to the craft sale.
(*Jeremy exits left.*)

(*In the churchyard.*)
(*Michael and Jeremy enter center.*)
Michael: Hi, Jeremy. What's in the sack?

Jeremy: Just a few things I brought for the church craft sale.

Michael: Let's see.

Jeremy: They're nothing, really.

Michael: Come on, don't be modest. Show me. (*Michael looks in Jeremy's bag.*) Wow! Those are neat. I'll bet they will sell right away. People go for things like that.

Jeremy: I hope so. I really want to help raise money to relieve world hunger. Where are your pipe-cleaner animals?

Michael: Grandma already took them to the craft room. She didn't want me to carry them. She was afraid I'd trip and squash them flat.

Jeremy: Sounds like something I'd do.

Michael: You can't be clumsy to have made beautiful plaques like those.

Jeremy: Well, I didn't exactly . . .

Michael: Oops, got to go! Grandma is waving for me to come inside.

(*Michael exits right.*)

Jeremy: I guess it doesn't make a big difference if Michael thinks I made the plaques. Calvin goes to a different church, so no one will know I didn't make them.

(*Jeremy exits center.*)

(*At the craft sale.*)

(*Michael and Jeremy enter center.*)

Michael: How's it going?

Jeremy: Great. People bought all my plaques. The last one sold while I was out in the hall getting a drink. I raised twelve dollars for the church. Isn't that great?

Michael: Sure is. We still have a few pipe-cleaner animals left, but they're going fast. Grandma's really pleased.

(*Michael exits center.*)

(*Jenny enters left.*)

Jenny: Want some fudge?

Jeremy: Sure.

Jenny: Ten cents a square.

Jeremy: You should give fudge to your brother free.

Jenny: Why? I had to pay for your plaque.

Jeremy: What do you mean?

Jenny: I bought your last plaque. I thought it was so pretty I'm going to give it to Connie for her birthday next week.

Jeremy: Connie?

Jenny: Yeah, you know. Connie, Calvin's sister.

Jeremy: Uh, but you can't do that.

Jenny: Why?

Jeremy: Because, well, uh, Connie might not, that is, ah, Connie is allergic to anything made with wood.

Jenny: Don't be silly! They live in a wood house.

Jeremy: She's, ah, allergic to the kind of paint I used, that's it.

Jenny: I'll wrap the plaque in plastic, so she won't have to touch or smell the paint.

Jeremy: No! You can't give it to her at all.

Jenny: You're acting really strange, Jeremy. Of course, I'm going to give it to her. Now, do you want this fudge for ten cents, or don't you?

Jeremy: No. I'm beginning to feel sick.

(Jenny shakes her head at his strange behavior and exits left.)

Jeremy: What am I going to do? If Jennie gives that plaque to Connie, Calvin will find out I took his plaques. Maybe he didn't really want me to have them after all. Why didn't I ask him before I took them? What am I going to do?

(Jeremy exits center.)

(At Jeremy's house.)

(Calvin enters center.)

Calvin: Knock, knock.

(Dad enters right.)

Dad: Hi, Calvin. If you're looking for Jeremy, he's not here.

Calvin: Maybe you can help me. I made twenty wooden plaques with Scripture verses on them for Christmas presents. Four of them are missing. You didn't see anyone near my garage, did you?

Dad: No, I just got home from a business meeting. I'm sorry to
hear they're missing. If I spot them, I'll tell you.

Calvin: Thanks. I sure hope I get them back soon. I don't have
time to make four more plaques before Christmas.

(*Calvin exits center. Dad exits right.*)

(*Jeremy enters center.*)

Jeremy: I know what I have to do. I have to steal that plaque from
Jenny before she can give it to Connie. I know Jenny came
home from the craft sale already. Then she left again to go
shopping with Mom. Maybe she put the plaque in her room.

(*Jeremy moves toward right and looks around.*)

Jeremy: Aha, here it is in her top drawer. I'll hide it on the top
shelf of my closet. No one will find it there.

(*Jeremy exits center.*)

(*At Jeremy's house.*)

(*Jenny enters left. Jeremy enters center.*)

Jenny: Hi, Jeremy.

Jeremy: Hi.

Jenny: I met Connie at the shopping center.

Jeremy: Connie who?

Jenny: Connie, Calvin's sister, you nerd.

Jeremy: Oh, that Connie!

Jenny: You know what she said?

Jeremy: No.

Jenny: She said she's not allergic to wood or paint. She can't
figure out where you got such a dumb idea. In fact, she said
she's been helping Calvin with a wood-and-paint project all
month.

Jeremy: Oh, really?

Jenny: Yes, really.

Jeremy: Well, maybe I misunderstood Calvin. I thought he told
me his sister was allergic to wood and paint.

Jenny: I bought some pretty wrapping paper. I'm going to my
room now to wrap Connie's present.

(*Jenny exits right.*)

Jeremy: I've got to get out of here before she finds that plaque is missing. (*Calls out.*) Dad, can I ride my bike in the park?

Dad (*from offstage*): Sure, Son. Be home in time for supper.

Jeremy: OK.

(*Jeremy exits center.*)

(*Jenny enters right, very agitated.*)

Jenny: It's gone!

(*Dad enters left.*)

Dad: What's gone, Honey?

Jenny: The plaque I bought at the craft sale. It was in my top drawer, and now it's gone!

Dad: What did it look like?

Jenny: It was made of wood, and it had a Scripture verse painted on it.

Dad: That's strange.

Jenny: No, it isn't. It's really neat.

Dad: I don't mean the plaque is strange. I mean, Calvin came over here earlier today and said someone took four plaques just like you described from his garage.

Jenny: Four plaques?

Dad: Yeah.

Jenny: Four plaques!

Dad: That's what I said.

Jenny: Four plaques!

Dad: You want me to spell it for you?

Jenny: Things are beginning to add up.

Dad: What are you talking about?

Jenny: Jeremy took four plaques to the craft sale to sell. I bought one, and when I told him I was going to give it to Calvin's sister as a birthday present, he got all upset. He told me I couldn't because she was allergic to wood and paint.

Dad: Maybe she is.

Jenny: But I met her at the shopping mall today, and she told me she wasn't allergic to anything. She also said she's been helping her brother with a wood-and-paint project all month.

Dad: What are you trying to say?

Jenny: I'm saying Jeremy took those plaques so he'd have something to sell at the craft sale.

Dad: That's a pretty serious accusation.

Jenny: I'm also saying he stole my plaque so I wouldn't give it to Connie.

Dad: Now, wait a minute, Jenny! Aren't you jumping to a few too many conclusions?

Jenny: I don't think so.

Dad: You'd better have some proof before you say things like that. You could ruin someone's reputation by accusing him of things he didn't do.

Jenny: I'll get proof. If Jeremy took that plaque, I know where it is.

Dad: Where?

Jenny: On the top shelf of his closet. That's where he puts all the stuff he doesn't want anyone to find.

Dad: And how do you know that?

Jenny: I watched him hide the Christmas presents he bought last year. That's where he put them all.

Dad: Snoopy, aren't you?

Jenny: Sometimes it pays to be snoopy.

Dad: Let's go look. But if the plaque isn't there, you have some apologizing to do.

(*Both exit center, then reenter.*)

Dad: You were right. The plaque was just where you said it would be. I'll have a talk with Jeremy when he gets home.

(*Jeremy enters left.*)

Jeremy: Hi, Dad. Oh, uh, hi, Jenny.

Jenny: You're in big trouble, Buster!

Dad: Jenny, you keep out of this! Where did you get this plaque, Son?

Jeremy: What's that?

Jenny: Oh, brother, now he's going to lie about it.

Dad: Jenny, I'm warning you; keep out of this!

Jeremy: Oh, that plaque! I, uh, I made it.

Dad: When did you have time to do that, Son? Just two days ago

you were asking me to help you make a craft project. You
couldn't have done this in two days.

Jeremy: But I did.

Jenny: You're just making things worse, Jeremy.

Dad: I told you to keep out of this, Jenny.

Jeremy: Yeah, bug off.

Dad: If you made this, Jeremy, there should be some paint cans
with this color paint somewhere in the house. You bring them
to me, and I'll believe you made the plaque.

Jeremy: I can't do that.

Jenny: Because you didn't make the plaque, that's why!

Dad: Be quiet, Jenny. Why can't you show me the paint cans,
Son?

Jeremy: Because, ah, because I threw them away, that's it.

Dad: Did you put them in the trash can?

Jeremy: Yeah, the one in the garage.

Dad: It should be easy enough to check your story. The garbage
hasn't been picked up yet this week. So if you put the paint
cans in there, they'll still be there. Let's go look.

Jeremy: Oh, well. You might as well know. It's true. I didn't
make the plaque.

Dad: Then where did you get it?

Jeremy: From Calvin.

Dad: What do you mean, from Calvin?

Jeremy: He gave it to me. Well, I mean, he sort of did.

Dad: Don't you think it's time you told me the whole story?

Jenny: What a creepy brother! You're a thief and a lousy liar.

Dad: That's enough, Jenny! Go to your room right now.

Jenny: But, Dad!

Dad: Now, young lady!

(*Jenny exits right in a huff.*)

Dad: Better tell me what happened.

Jeremy: Well, see, Calvin showed me these neat plaques he made.
Then he had to leave, and he told me I could stay and look
at them. I didn't think he'd mind if I took four to sell at the
church craft sale. So I took them because I wanted to help

raise money for the world hunger cause. But I guess it wasn't the right thing to do after all.

Dad: You're right about that. Why did you take the plaque Jenny bought?

Jeremy: She was going to give it to Connie. If I let her do that, Calvin would know I took his plaques.

Dad: He was over here earlier today asking if I'd seen anyone near his garage because four of his plaques were missing. He was pretty worried.

Jeremy: I've ruined everything. After I took those plaques, nothing worked right. I had to steal and lie, but everything fell apart anyway. It was terrible.

Dad: It's not over yet!

Jeremy: I know. I still have to tell Calvin. He'll probably never speak to me again.

Dad: And besides that, you're going to have to help him replace those plaques you took. He won't have time to make four more before Christmas by himself.

Jeremy: But I can't make neat letters like Calvin does.

Dad: Maybe you can do his chores so he has more time to work on the plaques.

Jeremy: Chores?

Dad: Sure, like helping his parents vacuum the rug, clean the toilets, and take out the garbage.

Jeremy: But, Dad . . .

Dad: You owe it to Calvin, don't you think?

Jeremy: I guess so. But I hate to clean toilets.

Dad: Besides doing Calvin's chores, you have more fence mending to do.

Jeremy: I do?

Dad: What about your sister?

Jeremy: Oh, yeah. Well, I guess I'll have to give her the three dollars she paid for that plaque since Calvin will want it back.

Dad: And?

Jeremy: And tell her I'm sorry for taking it from her room.

Dad: Once you've done that, I think you'll have all your fence
    mending done.
Jeremy: I'll never take something that doesn't belong to me again.
    It's not worth all the problems it causes.
Dad: If you've learned that, Son, you've learned a big, big lesson.
    Come on, let's start mending fences with Jenny.
(*Jeremy and Dad exit center.*)

14
Your Friend Tells You to Cheat or Lose His Friendship

Scripture: Numbers 23:11-12
Props: Three test papers
Performance Time: 8 minutes
Characters: Gordon, Frank, Gerald, Donna, Mrs. Jones

(*On the playground after school.*)
(*Gordon and Frank enter center.*)
Gordon: Ready for the big social studies test tomorrow?
Frank: I think so. I studied pretty hard last night.
Gordon: I was going to, but there was a really good movie on TV, so I watched it instead.
Frank: Uh oh!
Gordon: I'm not worried.
Frank: You ought to be. You got an *F* on your last two tests.
Gordon: That was before the teacher changed our seating arrangement.
Frank: What does that have to do with anything?
Gordon: Now I'm sitting beside you.
Frank: So?
Gordon: So you can let me copy off your paper.
Frank: Are you asking me to help you cheat?
Gordon: Sure. We're best friends, aren't we?
Frank: We go back four years, ever since you moved to town. But I can't help you cheat. It wouldn't be right.
Gordon: Come on, Frank. Don't be such a goody-two-shoes. Ev-

erybody does it. Just keep your hand away from your paper
every once in a while, so I can copy your answers.

Frank: Sorry, Gordon, I can't do that.

Gordon: You jerk! You're no friend. You're a lousy traitor.

Frank: No, I'm not.

Gordon: You are too.

Frank: I am not. I'm trying to do you a favor by keeping you out
of trouble.

Gordon: If you think I believe that, you're nuts.

Frank: The trouble with you is you're lazy.

Gordon: And you're Mr. Perfect who gets As and Bs all the time.
You make me sick.

Frank: If you studied, you'd get good grades too.

Gordon: Remember the birthday party my parents have for me
every year?

Frank: Yeah. The last one was really neat. The whole neighborhood came, and we played a lot of fun games.

Gordon: Well, my birthday party is next Tuesday, and you can
forget about coming. If you don't help me cheat, you're no
friend of mine, and only my friends are invited.

Frank: You really know how to hurt a guy.

Gordon: So will you help me cheat?

Frank: I can't.

Gordon: OK for you, Mr. Perfect. Don't come to me for any
favors. Stay out of my life from now on.

(Gordon exits center.)

(Gerald enters left.)

Gerald: What's wrong? You look like you've lost your best friend.

Frank: I have. Gordon's mad at me.

Gerald: Why?

Frank: I won't help him copy from my paper during tomorrow's
social studies test.

Gerald: Why not let him?

Frank: It wouldn't be fair. Tests are supposed to show how much
you know, not how well you can copy someone else's paper.

Gerald: Gordon never stays mad long. Give him time. He'll cool off.

Frank: No, he won't.

Gerald: You just watch.

Frank: He says he doesn't want to ever see me again, and he's not going to invite me to his birthday party.

Gerald: Uh oh! I guess he really is mad.

Frank: Yep.

Gerald: I'd hate to miss Gordon's birthday party. His dad is so funny. Remember the time he did his magician act?

Frank: Yeah, he was good.

Gerald: And that trick he taught us last year was really neat.

Frank: The code game?

Gerald: Yeah, where you say a word, and its first letter is the first letter of a special code word everyone else is supposed to guess.

Frank: And you keep saying words until you've spelled the code word.

Gerald: I even remember what the code word was.

Frank: Me too. It was *cane.*

Gerald: Remember the clues?

Frank: I sure do. They were chair, apple, nail, and elephant.

Gerald: Who finally figured out that the first letter of each word was the clue?

Frank: No one. Gordon's dad had to tell us.

Gerald: It's a neat code. I've used it several times since for other situations. Like when my sister and I don't want Mom and Dad to know what we're talking about.

Frank: Me too.

Gerald: If we do anything really neat at Gordon's birthday party this year, I'll tell you about it.

Frank: Thanks. I'll really miss not going.

(*Gerald exits left.*)

(*Donna enters right.*)

Donna: There you are, Frank. I've been looking all over for you.

Frank: You have?

Donna: Yeah.

Frank: Why?

Donna: You lent me your pencil in class today. I forgot to give it back. Here!

Frank: Thanks.

Donna: You sound sad.

Frank: I am a little.

Donna: Why?

Frank: Gordon says he won't be my friend anymore or invite me to his birthday party unless I help him cheat on the social studies test tomorrow.

Donna: There's an easy solution to that.

Frank: What?

Donna: Help him cheat.

Frank: I can't do that!

Donna: Just kidding. He's not much of a friend if he wants you to do something wrong, is he?

Frank: Maybe not.

Donna: So turn him in to the principal. That'll teach him.

Frank: I don't want to make trouble for him.

Donna: He's causing you a lot of grief, isn't he? Turnabout's fair play.

Frank: I'd hate to have him feel as badly as I do now.

Donna: Well, I'm glad it's not my problem.

(*Donna exits right, Frank exits center.*)

(*In class the next day.*)

(*Gordon and Frank enter center.*)

Gordon: Are you going to let me copy from you?

Frank: What you do with what you can see is your business.

Gordon: Hey, thanks, pal. You can come to my birthday party.

(*Gordon and Frank sit down.*)

Gordon: Why do you have two test papers?

Frank: Shhh.

Gordon: I can only see one well enough to copy from it.

Frank: Hush, or you'll get us both in trouble.

(Gordon copies what he can see from Frank, then both hand in their papers.)
Gordon: Thanks, Frank. I would have gotten an *F* for sure without you.
Frank: Don't thank me until you get your test back.
Gordon: I'm not worried. You always get good grades.
(Gordon and Frank exit center.)

(Next day in class.)
(Mrs. Jones enters right, Frank and Gordon enter center.)
Mrs. Jones: Frank, this is an excellent paper. *(Hands Frank his test paper.)*
Frank: Thanks.
Mrs. Jones: Gordon, I want you to stay after school.
Gordon: Why?
Mrs. Jones: I need to discuss your paper with you.
Gordon: Oh. Uh, well, OK. How'd I do on the test?
Mrs. Jones: We'll discuss it after school.
(Frank and Gordon exit center, Mrs. Jones exits right.)

(After school in the classroom.)
(Mrs. Jones enters right, Gordon enters center.)
Gordon: Well, here I am.
Mrs. Jones: There's something peculiar about your test paper.
Gordon: What's that?
Mrs. Jones: The answers have nothing to do with the questions. And the first letter of each answer forms a message.
Gordon: It does?
Mrs. Jones: Yes. There are eight questions. The answer to your first question begins with *I*. The answer to the second question begins with *C*, and it goes on down the page until you've spelled the message: "I cheated."
Gordon: Why, that little tramp!
Mrs. Jones: Just who are you calling a tramp?
Gordon: Uh, no one. That's just an, uh, an expression.
Mrs. Jones: I don't need to tell you that you got an *F.*

Gordon: I guessed that.

Mrs. Jones: But I'm feeling generous today, so I'll let you make up the test if you want to.

Gordon: Really? Thanks, Mrs. Jones. You're swell.

Mrs. Jones: There's only one catch.

Gordon: What's that?

Mrs. Jones: You must make it up next Tuesday night.

Gordon: Tuesday! But that's my birthday. My parents have been planning a big party for weeks.

Mrs. Jones: Take your choice. Make up the test or get an *F.*

Gordon: No fair. Can't you change the date?

Mrs. Jones: No.

Gordon: Please?

Mrs. Jones: No, Gordon.

Gordon: But you don't understand.

Mrs. Jones: You're the one who doesn't seem to understand. Do you or don't you want a second chance?

Gordon: If I get an *F* on this test, I'll flunk social studies. I have to take the test again.

Mrs. Jones: Then I'll see you here Tuesday night.

(*Mrs. Jones exits right.*)

Gordon: Wait till I get my hands on that jerk, Frank. I'll kill him for ruining my birthday party.

(*Gordon exits center.*)

(*Tuesday night in class.*)

(*Gordon enters center, Mrs. Jones enters right.*)

Gordon: I'm finally finished, Mrs. Jones.

Mrs. Jones: Bring the test to me. I'll grade it right now.

Gordon: I really studied hard for this.

Mrs. Jones: Gordon, I'm proud of you. You got a *B* plus.

Gordon: I did?

Mrs. Jones: See, you don't need to cheat to get good grades.

Gordon: It really feels good to do well all by myself.

Mrs. Jones: I'm glad you've finally learned that. By the way, there's someone here to see you.

Gordon: Who?

(*Frank enters left.*)

Gordon: Oh, it's you!

(*Gerald and Donna enter left.*)

Frank: And Gerald and Donna.

Gordon: What are you doing here? You're supposed to be at my birthday party, which is going on without me.

Donna: Since you couldn't come, we arranged to bring the party to you.

Gordon: You brought the party to school?

Mrs. Jones: I think you have a party to attend, Gordon. You'd better get going. I believe I heard party noises coming from the gym.

Gordon: Did you know about this?

Mrs. Jones: Who do you think got permission for your party to be in the gym?

Gordon: You mean you and Frank cooked all this up?

Frank: Yes. Mrs. Jones let me turn in two test papers, the real one and the one you copied. I used that code trick your dad taught us at your birthday party last year to make you spell "I cheated."

Gordon: I can't believe I fell for it. I should be furious with you, but I'm not. You did me a favor. Now I know how good it feels to get good grades by myself.

Mrs. Jones: Good for you, Gordon. I'd say you have some pretty good friends.

Gordon: You're the best friend I ever had, Frank. Sorry I was so mean to you.

Frank: That's OK.

Gerald: I'm hungry. How about some ice cream and cake?

Donna: Yeah, come on, let's go to the gym. Gordon's dad is there with some crazy contraption. I'm dying to see what he's got up his sleeve this year.

(*Mrs. Jones exits right, Gerald, Donna, Frank, and Gordon exit left.*)

15
You're Criticized by the Person You Helped

Scripture: Matthew 7:1-3
Props: Cardboard tube, picture of cat, apple (All can be imaginary.)
Performance Time: 4 minutes
Characters: Karla, Alice, Bert

(*On the sidewalk.*)
(*Karla and Alice enter right.*)
Karla: That tube looks heavy. Do you need help carrying it?
Alice: No.
Karla: What is it? A telescope or something?
Alice: It's a cat poster. I can hardly wait to hang it on my bedroom wall.
Karla: Can I help?
Alice: Sure. Come home with me, and we'll hang it up together.
Karla: OK! Then I won't have to see my brother quite so soon. The less I have to put up with bratty Bert, the better.
Alice: What did he do now?
Karla: When he was helping me clean off the breakfast table this morning, he tripped and spilled a whole box of cereal on the floor. He's so clumsy.
Alice: Brothers can be a real pain.
Karla: And how!
Alice: Here we are. Come on in. This is my room.
Karla: It's pretty.

Alice: I'll hang the poster above my dresser so I can see it when I lie in bed.

Karla: Let me help get the poster out of the tube.

Alice: Careful. I don't want it to tear.

(*Alice and Karla remove poster from tube.*)

Karla: There, it's out.

Alice: You hold the poster edges while I put tape on them.

Karla: OK.

Alice: Now, let's lift the whole thing up and tape it to the wall.

Karla: Heave, ho, let's go!

Alice: Careful!

Karla: Oops!

Alice: You ripped it!

Karla: No, I didn't.

Alice: It tore right by your hand.

Karla: I didn't mean to tear it.

Alice: I told you to be careful.

Karla: I'll mend it with some tape.

Alice: Just leave it alone. You're so clumsy you might make a bigger mess. I wish I hadn't asked you to help at all.

Karla: I said I was sorry.

Alice: Sorry won't fix my poster.

Karla: See if I ever help you again!

Alice: See if I ever ask you to.

Karla: If you're going to be so nasty about it, I'll leave.

Alice: Good riddance!

(*Karla exits right, Alice exits center.*)

(*At Karla's house.*)

(*Karla enters right, Bert enters center.*)

Bert: You're finally home. I thought you got lost or something.

Karla: Oh, be quiet!

Bert: I was starting to get worried.

Karla: Bug off, will you?

Bert: Are you still mad at me?

Karla: About what?

Bert: For spilling the cereal this morning.

Karla: Oh, that. I'd forgotten all about it. Why did you have to remind me?

Bert: Sorry. I was just trying to help.

Karla: You help yourself into more trouble than anyone I know, you clumsy clod.

Bert: If that's the way you feel, tomorrow I'll let you clean up the breakfast table all by yourself.

Karla: Good!

Bert: Want an apple?

Karla: I guess so.

Bert: Here.

Karla: Thanks.

Bert: See, brothers are good for something besides causing trouble.

Karla: You're OK—sometimes.

Bert: If you're not still mad about the cereal, why are you so upset?

Karla: Alice is mad at me again.

Bert: She's always mad about something. What's the matter this time?

Karla: I was helping her hang a cat poster on her wall. The poster tore, and she blamed me.

Bert: It hurts when you help someone and they criticize you, doesn't it?

Karla: Yeah, especially since I don't think it was my fault the poster tore.

Bert: Let her hang her own posters after this.

Karla: Oops, I just stepped on something crunchy.

Bert: What is it? A bug?

Karla: No, it's some of that cereal you spilled.

Bert: Oh.

Karla: There's a bunch of it on the floor over here. Pick it up.

Bert: Why me?

Karla: Because you spilled it.

Bert: I wouldn't have spilled it if you hadn't left your purse on the floor for me to trip over.

Karla: If you'd keep your eyes open, you wouldn't trip over everything in sight.

Bert: I was just trying to help, and look what kind of gratitude I get.

Karla: Oh, boy! Listen to us.

Bert: I am listening, and I wish you'd be quiet.

Karla: We sound just like Alice and me.

Bert: You two deserve each other.

Karla: I guess I have been acting pretty creepy.

Bert: I'm used to it. You're always hollering at me about something.

Karla: I am?

Bert: Every time I try to help, you blame me for doing it wrong.

Karla: I do?

Bert: Yeah. Sometimes I wonder why I keep helping you.

Karla: I'm sorry, Bert. I didn't know I acted that way.

Bert: Well, you do—every single day.

Karla: I guess Alice did me a favor by showing me just how bad it hurts when someone criticizes you after you try to help.

Bert: Maybe she's good for something after all. Here, I'll pick up the cereal.

Karla: I'll help.

Bert: I like this lots better than fighting.

Karla: Me too. If we really work at it, we might make a pretty good team.

(*Bert and Karla exit center.*)